BOOKKEEPING
THE
EASY WAY

BOOKKEEPING
THE
EASY WAY

WALLACE W. KRAVITZ

Publishers' Editorial Consultant for Business Education
Formerly Business Education Chairman
Mineola High School
Mineola, New York

Barron's Educational Series, Inc.
New York / London / Toronto / Sydney

All inquires should be addressed to:
Barron's Educational Series, Inc.
250 Wireless Boulevard
Hauppauge, New York 11788

Library of Congress Catalog Card No. 83-7069
International Standard Book No. 0-8120-2622-5

Library of Congress Cataloging in Publication Data
Kravitz, Wallace W.
   Bookkeeping the easy way.

   Includes index.
   1. Bookkeeping.   I. Title.
HF5635.K87 1983   657'.2   83-7069
ISBN 0-8120-2622-5

PRINTED IN THE UNITED STATES OF AMERICA

890   100   16 15 14 13 12 11

CONTENTS

Preface   ix

CYCLE ONE   A PERSONAL/SERVICE-TYPE BUSINESS

Chapter 1   Assets, Liabilities, and Owner's Equity   3
Definition of Assets   3
Examples of Assets—Personal and Business   3
Definition of Liabilities   4
Examples of Liabilities—Personal and Business   4
Definition of Owner's Equity   5
Examples of Owner's Equity   5
The Fundamental Bookkeeping Equation:
    Assets = Liabilities + Owner's Equity   5
Variations of the Fundamental Equation   6

Chapter 2   Business Transactions and Changes in the
                Fundamental Bookkeeping Equation   9
Transactions Increasing Accounts   10
Transactions Decreasing Accounts   10
Transactions That Increase and Decrease Accounts   11

Chapter 3   The Balance Sheet   15
Purpose, Form, and Content   15
Fundamental Bookkeeping Equation   16
Changes in Owner's Equity   17

Chapter 4   The Ledger   23
"T" Form of Accounts—Ruled Forms, Debit and Credit   23
Opening Account Balances   24
Rules for Increases/Decreases in Assets, Liabilities, and Owner's Equity   24
Proving the Equality of Debits and Credits   25

Chapter 5   Owner's Equity Accounts   31
Revenue Accounts for Income Earned   31
Expenses   31
Net Income/Net Loss   31
Effect of Revenue/Expenses on Owner's Equity   32
Owner's Drawing Account   32
Effect of Withdrawal on Owner's Equity   33

Chapter 6 Two-Column General Journal   **39**
Book of Original Entry   39
Source Documents   40
Journalizing   42

Chapter 7 Posting the General Journal   **45**
Posting Procedure   45
  Journal to Ledger   46
  Cross Referencing   47
Trial Balance   47

Chapter 8 The Trial Balance and Work Sheet   **55**
Locating Errors   55
Errors That the Trial Balance Does Not Reveal   56
The Six-Column Work Sheet   56

Chapter 9 Financial Statements   **63**
Income Statement—Form and Content   63
Capital Statement   64
Balance Sheet—Form and Content   66

Chapter 10 Closing the Ledger   **73**
Revenue and Expense Summary   73
Accounts Closed/Accounts Open—Ruling, Balancing   76

Chapter 11 Cash Systems, Checking Accounts   **91**
Opening a Checking Account   91
Endorsing Checks   91
Making Deposits   92
Drawing Checks   93
The Bank Statement   94
Reconciling Check Stub Balance and Bank Statement   94

Chapter 12 The Petty Cash Fund   **101**
Purpose of the Fund   101
Establishing the Fund   101
Making Disbursements   102
Proving Petty Cash   103
Replenishing the Fund   103

Cycle One Examination   **109**

CYCLE TWO   A MERCHANDISING BUSINESS

Chapter 13 Purchases of Merchandise   **119**
Purchasing on Account—Accounts Payable   119
Purchases Journal   119
Posting Creditors' Accounts   120
Summarizing the Purchases Journal   120
Schedule of Accounts Payable   122

Chapter 14 Cash Disbursements Journal **129**
Columnar Journal—Special Columns 129
Summarizing the Journal 130
Schedule of Accounts Payable 132
Source Document for Cash Disbursement 133

Chapter 15 Sales of Merchandise **137**
Sales on Account 137
Sales Journal and Accounts Receivable Ledger 137
Source Documents for Sales Journal Entries 138
Posting and Summarizing the Sales Journal 138
Schedule of Accounts Receivable 140

Chapter 16 Cash Receipts Journal **147**
Purpose of Cash Receipts Journal 147
Posting to Accounts 148
Summarizing the Cash Receipts Journal 148
Schedule of Accounts Receivable 151
Expanding the Journal 151
Source Documents for Cash Receipts 152

Chapter 17 General Journal, Four-Column Format **159**
Sales Returns and Allowances, and Purchases Returns and Allowances 159
Source Documents 160
Correcting Errors in Ledger Postings 161
Statement of Account 162

Chapter 18 Eight-Column Work Sheet **171**
Trial Balance 171
Adjusting Entries 171
Merchandise Inventory 172
Supplies 172
Other Prepaid Expenses 172
Extending Updated Balances 172
Determining Net Income or Net Loss 172

Chapter 19 Financial Statements **183**
Income Statement 184
Capital Statement 185
Balance Sheet 187

Chapter 20 Adjusting and Closing the General Ledger **197**
Adjusting Accounts 197
Closing Accounts 199
Post-closing Trial Balance 200

Cycle Two Examination **207**

Answers to Selected Questions and Problems **219**
Index **261**

PREFACE

Bookkeeping the Easy Way presents a simplified step-by-step approach to learning book-keeping/accounting principles and practices. Understanding basic bookkeeping procedures is vital to developing an understanding of more advanced accounting theory and practice. There-fore, mastering the concepts of double-entry bookkeeping is a prerequisite to any further study.

This text is designed to be used in a variety of ways, depending on the need of the learner.

(1) Those who wish to study independently, at their own pace, will find this presentation clear and concise, without distractions.
(2) Those enrolled in adult education or continuing education courses will find that this text is designed for a relaxed, successful learning experience.
(3) Those who wish to study this subject in a one-semester course will find this work ideally arranged to coincide with most school half-year time schedules.
(4) Those who are having difficulty in grasping the fundamentals in a traditional introductory course in bookkeeping or accounting will find the text ideal for review or for remedial study.

Bookkeeping the Easy Way presents basic material for the individual, family, or sole proprietorship—a business owned by one person, typical of many business organizations. With improved bookkeeping skills, each individual, family, or business will gain a better command of available resources and help in planning a more profitable future.

Each chapter introduces one or two basic concepts of bookkeeping/accounting. Suc-ceeding chapters build on the work that is covered in the preceding chapters. None can be omitted, nor should the order be changed. At the end of each chapter, students will find questions and problems, as well as analytical situations designed to explain not only the "how" but also—and equally important—the "why" of bookkeeping practices. These situations relate book learning to the business world. Including this work will result in a better understanding of legal obligations, a greater awareness of the private enterprise system, and, for learners, a career exploration experience.

I would like to acknowledge the invaluable and inspirational aid of my wife, Mollie S. Kravitz, in helping with editorial work, as well as the typing of the original manuscript.

WALLACE W. KRAVITZ

CYCLE ONE
A Personal/Service-Type Business

CHAPTER 1

ASSETS, LIABILITIES, AND OWNER'S EQUITY

The fundamental elements of all bookkeeping systems deal with keeping records for changes that occur in ASSETS, LIABILITIES, and OWNER'S EQUITY.

Definition of Assets

ASSETS are all things of value owned by an individual or business. Personal assets may include cash on hand, as well as savings and checking accounts, an automobile, and a home. Business assets may include similar items, as well as amounts due from customers—ACCOUNTS RECEIVABLE—and a building owned, not rented.

Examples of Assets—Personal and Business

A high school student's personal assets might include the following:

    Cash on hand and in a savings account
    Clothing
    Sporting equipment
    Jewelry
    Bicycle

A family's personal assets might include the following:

Cash on hand, savings, and checking account
Home owned, not rented
Furniture and furnishings
Investments in stocks, bonds, and/or land

The assets of a small service-type business might include the following:

Cash on hand and in checking accounts
Building owned, not rented
Equipment
Supplies
Delivery truck

Consider the following list of assets used by the Evergreen Landscaping Service, a company owned by Thomas Morales:

Cash	$ 1,450
Truck	11,000
Haulaway Trailer	1,500
Customers' Accounts	3,600
Equipment	3,320
Office Furniture	750
Supplies	645
Total Assets	$22,265

Customers' accounts, the amounts due to be collected in a short time, are assets because they represent amounts that will be turned into cash as they are received. These are ACCOUNTS RECEIVABLE, and will be referred to by that term in this text.

Definition of Liabilities

LIABILITIES are the debts owed by an individual or business. Personal liabilities may include unpaid charge account balances, as well as amounts owed on a home and/or automobile loan. Business liabilities may include similar items: amounts owed, or ACCOUNTS PAYABLE.

Examples of Liabilities—Personal and Business

A high school student's personal liabilities might include the following:

Loan from parents to purchase car
Balance owed on school yearbook or class ring

A family's personal liabilities might include the following:

Balance owed on home mortgage
Balance owed on installment purchases
Unpaid household bills—gas, electric, telephone

Consider the following list of liabilities owed by the Evergreen Landscaping Service:

Truck Loan, Island National Bank	$6,200
Supplies Bought on Account	345
Equipment Bought on Account	1,000
Total Liabilities	$7,545

Definition of Owner's Equity

OWNER'S EQUITY is the net worth or capital of an individual or business. It is the amount of assets remaining after all liabilities are paid. To determine an individual's or family's owner's equity, total all assets, then deduct all liabilities. The difference is the owner's equity.

Examples of Owner's Equity

If a high school student's assets total $2,675, and liabilities total $450, the student's owner's equity equals $2,225:

Total Assets	$2,675
Less Total Liabilities	450
Owner's Equity	$2,225

If a family's assets total $103,700, and liabilities total $44,960, the family's owner's equity equals $60,740:

Total Assets	$103,700
Less Total Liabilities	44,960
Owner's Equity	$ 60,740

To determine Thomas Morales's owner's equity, follow the same calculation:

Total Assets	$22,265
Less Total Liabilities	7,545
Owner's Equity	$14,720

Owner's equity is frequently referred to as NET WORTH, CAPITAL, or PROPRIETORSHIP. Individuals, however, usually refer to their owner's equity as "net worth" or "capital." A business might use all of these terms; however, this text will use most frequently OWNER'S EQUITY and CAPITAL.

The Fundamental Bookkeeping Equation

The relationship among the three elements of bookkeeping—assets, liabilities, and owner's equity—may be stated as follows:

> (1) ASSETS equal   (2) LIABILITIES plus   (3) OWNER'S EQUITY

Consider these in the following way:

ASSETS (everything of value *owned*)	LIABILITIES (all debts *owed*) plus OWNER'S EQUITY

An example of these three elements as they apply to Thomas Morales's truck is:

Truck

Original cost	$11,000	Balance owed to bank and Morales's equity in truck		$ 6,200
				4,800
Total	$11,000	Total		$11,000

These three elements of bookkeeping may be stated as an equation:

$$\text{Assets} = \text{Liabilities} + \text{Owner's Equity}$$
$$\$11,000 = \$6,200 + \$4,800$$

or, simply,

$$A = L + OE$$

If owner's equity is referred to as capital, the equation is restated as

$$A = L + C$$

Variations of the Fundamental Equation

When any two of the fundamental elements are known, the third can be found. If assets total $10,000 and liabilities total $4,000, owner's equity equals $6,000. Assets minus liabilities equal owner's equity, or

$$A - L = OE$$

If assets total $12,835 and owner's equity totals $7,000, liabilities equal $5,835. It is also true that assets minus owner's equity equal liabilities, or

$$A - OE = L$$

If liabilities total $16,000 and owner's equity totals $22,900, assets equal $38,900. It is also true that liabilities plus owner's equity equal assets. This reverses the sides of the fundamental bookkeeping equation:

$$L + OE = A$$

These examples illustrate the variations of the fundamental bookkeeping/accounting equation: $A = L + OE$. All of these are true statements, whether for an individual, a family, or a business.

YOU SHOULD REMEMBER

All assets are subject to *two* claims—those to whom debts are owed, and those of the owner(s).

In listing claims against assets, claims of those to whom debts are owed *always* come before claims of the owner(s).

KNOW YOUR VOCABULARY

Use each of the following words or terms in a statement relating to bookkeeping/accounting:

Accounts payable	Liabilities
Accounts receivable	Net worth
Asset(s)	Owner's equity
Capital	Proprietorship

QUESTIONS

Classify each of the following items by writing *Asset*, *Liability*, or *Owner's Equity* in the column at the right:

Item	Classification
Example: Cash on hand	Asset
1. Automobile	1. Asset
2. Balance owed on loan	2. Liability
3. Gerald Smith's capital	3. Equity
4. Supplies on hand	4. Asset
5. Personal clothes	5. Liability
6. Charge account balances	6. Liability
7. One's net worth	7. Owners Equity
8. Bank loan	8. Liability
9. Allison Paris, account receivable	9. Asset
10. Panos & George, account payable	10. Liability

PROBLEMS

1–1 Complete each of the fundamental bookkeeping equations so that each will be a true statement.

	Assets	= Liabilities	+ Owner's Equity
Example:	$ 10,500	$ 4,000	?($6,500)
1.	$ 15,750	$ 4,250	?11 500
2.	24,900	? 3700	$ 21,200
3.	? 7500	5,000	12,500
4.	24,742.50	8,655.40	?6087. 10
5.	31,070.92	? 8569.07	22,501.85
6.	175,882.35	68,951.39	?
7.	?	58,042.78	152,775.56
8.	229,953.11	?	189,638.63
9.	686,020.49	114,362.74	?
10.	?	330,172.41	786,570.87

(handwritten calculations in left margin:)
13
24742.50
8655.40
16087 10

10 6 8
28460.96
22501.85
8569 07

THINK IT OVER

Jack Calhoun's assets total $22,500; his liabilities total $7,500.

Mary Winslow's assets total $30,000; her owner's equity totals $25,000.

Which of these two individuals has a stronger "financial situation" or is better able to pay all debts owed? What other information might be needed in order to give a more definite answer?

WORDS TO REMEMBER
Account *each specific item* listed as either an asset, a liability, or an owner's equity
Business Transaction something that occurs, causing at least *two changes in accounts*
Investment a transaction made by an owner that *directly increases capital*, owner's equity

CHAPTER **2**

BUSINESS TRANSACTIONS AND CHANGES IN THE FUNDAMENTAL BOOKKEEPING EQUATION

REMEMBER:

$$A = L + OE$$

A BUSINESS TRANSACTION always results in at least two changes in the fundamental bookkeeping equation. Since both sides of this equation must be equal, a transaction that changes total assets must also change either total liabilities or total owner's equity.

Each item listed as either an asset, a liability, or an owner's equity is referred to as an ACCOUNT and is given a title—the Cash account, Truck account, Island National Bank account, Thomas Morales's Capital account, and so on.

Transactions Increasing Accounts

Assume that Morales, the owner of the Evergreen Landscaping Service, borrows $2,500 cash from the Island National Bank. The original bookkeeping equation showed:

$$\text{Assets} = \text{Liabilities} + \text{Owner's Equity}$$
$$\$22,265 = \$7,545 + \$14,720$$

With the cash borrowed, the equation changes because the asset account, Cash, increases and the liability account, Island National Bank, increases:

Assets	=	Liabilities	+ Owner's Equity
$22,265		$ 7,545	$14,720
+ 2,500		+ 2,500	----
$24,765 =		$10,045 +	$14,720

Because this transaction resulted in two account increases, total assets increased and total liabilities increased.

Assume that Morales takes $5,000 of his personal cash to make an additional IN-VESTMENT in this business. The equation now shows an increase in the Cash account and an increase in Thomas Morales's Capital account:

Assets	=	Liabilities	+ Owner's Equity
$24,765		$10,045	$14,720
+ 5,000		---	+ 5,000
$29,765 =		$10,045 +	$19,720

Because this transaction also resulted in two account increases, total assets increased and total owner's equity increased.

Transactions Decreasing Accounts

Assume that Morales pays $1,000 cash to the Island National Bank as part payment on the truck loan. The equation now shows a decrease in the Cash account and a decrease in the Island National Bank account:

Assets	=	Liabilities	+ Owner's Equity
$29,765		$10,045	$19,720
− 1,000		− 1,000	---
$28,765 =		$ 9,045 +	$19,720

Because this transaction resulted in two account decreases, total assets decreased and total liabilities decreased.

Transactions That Increase and Decrease Accounts

Some transactions may change two accounts on the *same side* of the equation without changing any totals. Assume that Morales bought $100 worth of supplies, paying cash for them. His Cash account decreased by $100, while his Supplies account increased by $100, with no change in total assets.

All transactions cause two (or more, as will be shown later) changes in accounts. These changes may result in

(1) two increases,
(2) two decreases, or
(3) one increase and one decrease.

When transactions result in two account increases or two account decreases, totals on both sides of the fundamental equation change:

	A	=	L	+	OE	
(1)	$10,000		$2,000		$8,000	
	+ 1,500		+ 1,500		---	(two increases)
	$11,500	=	$3,500	+	$8,000	
(2)	- 500		- 500		---	(two decreases)
	$11,000	=	$3,000	+	$8,000	
(3)	+ 350					(one increase,
	$11,350					
	- 350					one decrease)
	$11,000	=	$3,000	+	$8,000	

YOU SHOULD REMEMBER

All transactions cause at least two changes in accounts. Either:
—two accounts increase, or
—two accounts decrease, or
—one account increases, as one account decreases.

KNOW YOUR VOCABULARY

Use each of the following words or terms in a statement relating to bookkeeping/accounting:

Account   Investment
Business transaction

QUESTIONS

Classify each of the following accounts as an asset, liability, or owner's equity. Indicate on which side of the fundamental equation—left or right—each account would appear.

	Account	Classification	Side
Example:	Cash (checking account)	Asset	Left
1.	Delivery truck	1.	
2.	Account payable, J. Glover	2.	
3.	Paul Jacob, Capital	3.	
4.	Account receivable, K. Day	4.	
5.	Balance due J. C. Woolco	5.	
6.	Customer's account balance	6.	
7.	Equipment	7.	
8.	Balance owed on truck	8.	
9.	Stamp collection	9.	
10.	Proprietor's claim	10.	

PROBLEMS

2–1   Write the words *Increase* or *Decrease*, or both words, or *None*, to show any change(s) in TOTAL assets, liabilities, and owner's equity for each of the following transactions:

			A	=	L	+	OE
Example:	Owner invests cash in business.		Increase				Increase
1.	Paid balance due on loan.	1.					
2.	Paid cash for new calculator.	2.					
3.	Borrowed cash from bank.	3.					
4.	Received cash from customer.	4.					
5.	Sold old desk for cash.	5.					
6.	Transferred new desk from home to business.	6.					
7.	Bought new truck for cash.	7.					
8.	Withdrew cash for personal use.	8.					

2–2   For each of the following business transactions, add or subtract the amounts to update total assets, liabilities, and owner's equity:

Example: Karen Glaser, owner, invested $15,000 in a dry-cleaning business.

1. Bought $2,000 worth of equipment, paying cash.
2. Borrowed $7,500 from River National Bank.
3. Bought $450 worth of supplies, paying cash.
4. Bought a truck for $12,000, paying cash.
5. Made a $1,500 payment on loan to River National Bank.

	A	=	L	+	OE
Start with	$14,250		$4,250		$10,000
Example:	+ 15,000		---		+ 15,000
	$29,250		$4,250		$25,000
1.					
2.					
3.					
4.					
5.					

THINK IT OVER

Kenneth Lee operates a computer software business. He has a $16,000 cash balance. New equipment needed to develop the latest type of programs for his clients will cost $20,000. This will require some borrowing in order to pay for it. Lee wants to use $6,000 of cash from his business, arranging a bank loan for the balance.

What will be the amount of the loan? What changes will occur in the fundamental bookkeeping equation? Does Lee have any other choice in deciding how to buy this equipment?

CHAPTER 3

THE BALANCE SHEET

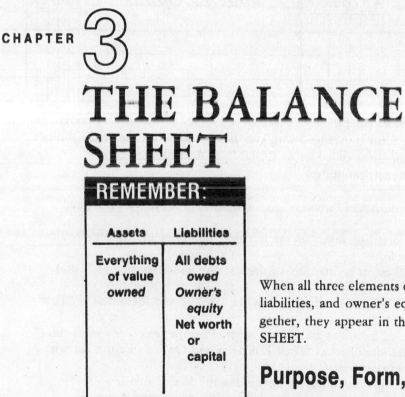

REMEMBER:

Assets	Liabilities
Everything of value owned	All debts owed Owner's equity Net worth or capital

When all three elements of bookkeeping—assets, liabilities, and owner's equity—are examined together, they appear in the form of a BALANCE SHEET.

Purpose, Form, and Content

A balance sheet is a financial statement or business form that lists, as of a certain date, all assets owned and all claims against these assets. These claims are held by CREDITORS, to whom money is owed, and the owners themselves, in the form of their owner's equity. When arranged in this way, it is easy to see that the fundamental bookkeeping equation again holds true:

$$A = L + OE$$

A bookkeeper or accounting clerk prepared a balance sheet for Thomas Morales's business on September 30, 198–.

15

Evergreen Landscaping Service
Balance Sheet
September 30, 198—

Assets		Liabilities	
Cash	7850|00	Gardners Supply Co.	345|00
Truck	11000|00	Equipment Mfg. Corp.	1000|00
Haulaway Trailer	1500|00	Island National Bank	7700|00
Accounts Receivable	3600|00	Total Liabilities	9045|00
Equipment	3320|00	Owner's Equity	
Office Furniture	750|00	Thomas Morales, Capital	19720|00
Supplies	745|00	Total Liabilities &	
Total Assets	28765|00	Owner's Equity	28765|00

This balance sheet shows the FINANCIAL CONDITION of Morales's business on the specified date. When this form is arranged with two sides—assets on the left, liabilities and owner's equity on the right—it is called an ACCOUNT FORM balance sheet.

Note the following details carefully:

(1) The heading consists of "answers" to the questions WHO, WHAT, and WHEN.
(2) The account form lists assets on the left side, liabilities and owner's equity on the right side.
(3) The sum of all assets is listed below the last one and identified as "Total Assets."
(4) The sum of all liabilities is listed below the last one and identified as "Total Liabilities."
(5) The sum of total liabilities and capital is listed on the *same line level* as the total assets and identified as "Total Liabilities and Owner's Equity" or with acceptable abbreviations.
(6) The final total dollar amounts on both sides are double ruled.
(7) The dollar symbol, comma, and decimal point are not used in any bookkeeping form or statement.

(Single ruled lines indicate an addition or subtraction. Double ruled lines indicate the end of the work.)

Fundamental Bookkeeping Equation

The fundamental bookkeeping equation is clearly seen on each balance sheet. The dollar value of total assets on the left side equals the dollar value of the creditors' claims (liabilities) plus capital (owner's equity) on the right side.

As shown earlier, each business transaction changes the dollar values of two items listed on the balance sheet. Therefore, a balance sheet showing a new financial condition, or picture, could be developed after each transaction. However, hundreds of transactions may occur daily, weekly, or monthly, making it impractical to do this so often. Usually financial statements are prepared at the end of a definite period of time—the FISCAL PERIOD. This can be monthly, quarterly, semimonthly, or annually. A 12-month fiscal period, however, need not coincide with the 12 calendar months of the year. A fiscal year could run from July 1 to the following June 30, or from April 1 to the following March 31.

Changes in Owner's Equity

Many of the transactions that occur during a fiscal period result in changes in owner's equity. These changes will eventually show up as increases or decreases in the owner's capital account. Even though the exact amount of change is not known, it can be determined by completing the fundamental bookkeeping equation. In completing the balance sheet for the Evergreen Landscaping Service, Morales's capital could have been calculated by subtracting total liabilities from total assets:

$$\$28,765 - \$9,045 = \$19,720 \quad \text{or} \quad A - L = OE$$

YOU SHOULD REMEMBER

Three items in a statement heading explain WHO, WHAT, and WHEN.
Assets *equal liabilities plus owner's equity*, or
Assets *minus liabilities equal owner's equity*.

KNOW YOUR VOCABULARY

Use each of the following words or terms in a statement relating to bookkeeping/accounting:

Account form	Creditor
Balance sheet	Financial condition
Claims against assets	Fiscal period

QUESTIONS

1. What three questions are answered in the heading of a balance sheet?
2. How many days are there in each month?
3. What is the last day of a quarterly fiscal period beginning on July 1? On January 1? On October 1?
4. What determines that a balance sheet is "in balance"?
5. How can owner's equity be found if total assets and total liabilities are known?
6. Write the following amounts in a ruled form, arranged for addition, and find the total: $7,650; $19,560; $835; $2,750; $182.

PROBLEMS

3–1 Identify each of the following items by writing *Asset*, *Liability*, or *Owner's Equity* in the column at the right:

Item		Classification
Example:	Cash on hand	Asset
1.	Automobile	1.
2.	Balance owed on time purchase	2.
3.	Cash in bank	3.
4.	Owner's claim against assets	4.
5.	Supplies for business use	5.
6.	Personal clothing	6.
7.	Unpaid balance on charge account	7.
8.	Creditor's claim against assets	8.
9.	Net worth	9.
10.	Money borrowed	10.

3–2 **Name the section of a balance sheet—Assets, Liabilities, or Owner's Equity—in which each of the following items should be located:**

			Balance Sheet	
			Left Side	Right Side
Example:	Machinery		Asset	
1.	Supplies	1.		
2.	Amounts owed to creditors	2.		
3.	Tools	3.		
4.	Bank loan	4.		
5.	Office equipment	5.		
6.	Checking account balance	6.		
7.	Amount due from customer	7.		
8.	Owner's financial claim	8.		
9.	Furniture	9.		
10.	Capital	10.		

3–3 On August 31 of the current year, the following assets and liabilities were listed by Maria Lopez, owner of Maria's Beauty Salon:

Assets:	Cash	$1,750
	Furniture and Fixtures	8,900
	Beauty Supplies	600
Liabilities:	Regal Laundry	275
	Marvelle Corp.	2,500

Prepare a balance sheet for Maria's Beauty Salon on the date indicated. Use the form in this chapter (page 16) for your model.

3–4 Paul Whitefeather, an accountant, has the following business assets and liabilities:

Assets:	Cash	$ 750
	Office Machines	3,500
	Furniture and Fixtures	3,150
	Office Supplies	285
Liabilities:	Kearney Evans Co.	650
	Cal's Stationery Co.	175

Prepare a balance sheet for Paul Whitefeather, dated September 30 of the current year.

3–5   The Dramatic Society of your local school has the following assets and liabilities on October 31 of the current year:

Assets:	Cash	$ 60.00
	Scenery	750.00
	Costumes	480.00
	Make-up Supplies	64.50
	Scripts	35.00
Liabilities:	E. Exter (seamstress)	75.00
	Field Lumber Co.	100.00
	Rex Drugstore	22.75

Prepare a balance sheet for the Dramatic Society on the date indicated. Indicate the owner's equity as Dramatic Society, Capital.

3–6   Lady Cake Bake Shoppe reports the following assets and liabilities on July 31 of the current year:

Assets:	Cash	$ 1,250.00
	Building	68,500.00
	Bakery Equipment	26,200.00
	Furniture and Fixtures	6,300.00
	Supplies	1,800.00
Liabilities:	Mortgage Loan Owed to Madison Bank	23,575.00
	Bakery Supplies Co.	350.00
	Baking Equipment Co.	5,000.00

Prepare a balance sheet for the Lady Cake Bake Shoppe on the date indicated. Gustave Mueller is the owner.

THINK IT OVER

Consider your own personal financial position. Prepare a list of all the assets you own. Place an estimated (or known) value on each. Do you owe any debts? What is your personal owner's equity? Prepare your own balance sheet, complete with heading.

Do the same for your family as a whole. Ask other members of the family for estimated values to place on all assets owned and all debts owed, if you are not certain of the amounts.

CHAPTER **4**

THE LEDGER

REMEMBER:

Assets =	Liabilities
	+
	Owner's
	equity

It is possible to record the changes each transaction causes by continually preparing new balance sheets. This "direct balance sheet" approach is not reasonable, however, because of the frequency of transactions and the amount of bookkeeping work involved. Furthermore, this does not provide a record that shows *how* each account changes; all that is shown is the final total in each account.

"T" Form of Accounts—Ruled Forms, Debit and Credit

To keep track of transactions and changes as they occur, a system of ACCOUNTS is used. The account form is used to record the changes that result in increases and decreases. Each item listed on a balance sheet is recorded in a separate account form. All accounts, taken together as one group, are called a LEDGER. The ruling for an account originates from the account form of a balance sheet: assets listed on the left side, liabilities and owner's equity on the right side.

Examine the Evergreen Landscaping Service's cash account, starting with an opening BALANCE of $1,450. (See page 4.) This account has a title: Cash. The left side of an account is the DEBIT side; the right side of an account is the CREDIT side.

Cash

1450

Each of the *assets* listed on page 4 would appear in the same way—as *debit balances*. Notice that they are in the form of an enlarged "T" and therefore are called T-ACCOUNTS.

23

Examine the T-account for Evergreen Landscaping Service's liability owed to Island National Bank. (See page 5.) This account has a title: Island National Bank. The left side is the debit side; the right side is the credit side.

Each of the *liabilities* listed on page 5 would appear in the same way—as a *credit balance*.

Examine Morales's owner's equity account: Thomas Morales, Capital. The account has a title: Thomas Morales, Capital.

The left side is the debit side; the right side is the credit side.

Opening Account Balances

Each account balance is opened by entering amounts on the proper debit or credit side. *Assets* are opened as *debits*, and any increases are placed on the debit side (for easy addition to obtain a total). *Liabilities* and *owner's equity* are opened as *credits*, and any increases are placed on the credit side.

Rules for Increases/Decreases in Assets, Liabilities, and Owner's Equity

The accepted bookkeeping/accounting abbreviations for debit and credit are Dr. and Cr., or dr. and cr. These are used in various business forms. Written statements will, however, use the complete words. Note carefully the following statements:

(1) *Assets* are accounts that appear on the left-hand side of a balance sheet and will show *increases* by *debits*.

(2) *Liabilities* are accounts that appear on the right-hand side of a balance sheet and will show *increases* by *credits*.

(3) *Owner's equity (capital)* appears on the right-hand side of a balance sheet and will show *increases* by *credits*.

Evergreen Landscaping Service's complete ledger has been opened from the account information listed on pages 4 and 5. Asset accounts are arranged first, followed by liabilities and owner's equity accounts.

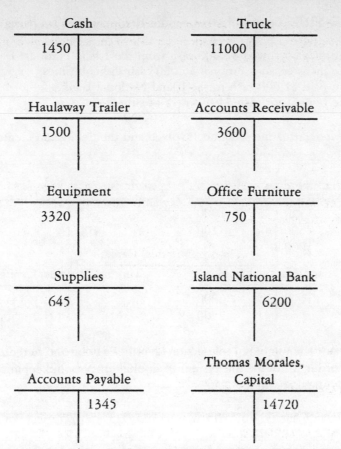

Cash	Truck
1450	11000

Haulaway Trailer	Accounts Receivable
1500	3600

Equipment	Office Furniture
3320	750

Supplies	Island National Bank
645	6200

Accounts Payable	Thomas Morales, Capital
1345	14720

Each account receivable could have been listed in a separate T-account to show the individual amount *due from each customer*. In the same way, each account payable could have been listed in a separate T-account to show the individual amount *owed to each creditor*. One creditor was listed in a separate account—Island National Bank. It could have been combined with the other accounts payable for one total amount owed—$7,545.

Because assets increase by debits, it follows that any *asset decreases* are recorded as *credits*. Because liabilities and owner's equity increase by credits, it follows that any *liability* and *owner's equity decreases* are recorded as *debits*. The three T-accounts shown on page 24 can now be completed to illustrate the RULES OF DEBITS AND CREDITS:

(1) Assets increase by debits and decrease by credits.
(2) Liabilities increase by credits and decrease by debits.
(3) Owner's equity increases by a credit and decreases by a debit.

Assets		Liabilities		Owner's Equity	
Dr.	Cr.	Dr.	Cr.	Dr.	Cr.
+	−	−	+	−	+

Proving the Equality of Debits and Credits

As transactions occur, changes are recorded in accounts. For every transaction, at least one account will be debited and one will be credited. Even though transactions change account balances, the fundamental bookkeeping/accounting equation will always be in balance: $A = L + OE$. This is the explanation of the theory of DOUBLE-ENTRY BOOKKEEPING: for every transaction debits always equal credits.

Reexamine in T-accounts the transactions first explained on pages 10 and 11:

(1) Morales borrowed $2,500 cash from the Island National Bank.
(2) He invested an additional $5,000 cash in his business.
(3) He paid $1,000 cash to the Island National Bank.
(4) He bought for cash $100 worth of supplies.

A *partial* ledger for the accounts involved and the debits and credits for (1), (2), (3), and (4) above is shown as follows:

	Cash				Supplies	
	1450	(3)	1000		645	
(1)	2500	(4)	100	(4)	100	
(2)	5000					

	Island National Bank			Thomas Morales, Capital		
(3)	1000		6200			14720
		(1)	2500		(2)	5000

Notice that each numbered transaction identifies a debit and a credit of equal amount. This is helpful in order to follow the system of double-entry bookkeeping. For every transaction, debits must equal credits.

YOU SHOULD REMEMBER

In every transaction debits equal credits.
Assets increase by debits and decrease by credits.
Liabilities increase by credits and decrease by debits.
Owner's equity increases by credits and decreases by debits.

KNOW YOUR VOCABULARY

Use each of the following words or terms in a statement relating to bookkeeping/accounting:

Account form   Double-entry bookkeeping

Balance   Ledger

Credit (cr.)   Rules of debits and credits

Debit (dr.)   T-account

QUESTIONS

1. Which of the following statements is true?
   a) For *every* transaction, the account(s) debited equal the account(s) credited.
   b) For *every* transaction, the account(s) increased equal the account(s) decreased.
2. Explain why the incorrect statement in Question 1 is not true.
3. What would be the normal balance of any asset account?
4. On which side—debit or credit—do accounts decrease?

PROBLEMS

4–1   Emilee Suzanne listed the following account balances:

Cash	$1,245
Equipment	3,670
Supplies	430
Accounts Payable:	
L. D. Brown	400
J. C. Tucker	175

(1)   Open a ledger of T-accounts for each of these accounts, including one for each creditor.

(2)   Open a T-account to record Emilee Suzanne's owner's equity. Remember: $A - L = OE$.

4–2   Paul Jacobs listed the following account balances:

Cash on Hand and in Bank	$1,305
Accounts Receivable:	
D. R. Able	150
M. O. Jackson	225
V. L. Witten	85
Truck	5,750
Supplies	395
Accounts Payable:	
City Trust Company	1,250
H. & H. Manufacturing Co.	800

(1)   Open a ledger of T-accounts for each account, including Jacobs's owner's equity.
(2)   Prove that Assets = Liabilities + Owner's Equity.

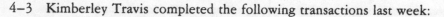

4–3   Kimberley Travis completed the following transactions last week:

Example: Paid Regal Bank, $150.
(1)   Bought $75 worth of supplies for cash.
(2)   Borrowed $1,000 from Regal Bank.
(3)   Invested $2,500 cash in her business.
(4)   Bought $500 worth of equipment from Bixby Company, agreeing to pay in 30 days.

Record the debits and credits for each of the above transactions in the following partial ledger. Beginning account balances are indicated. Identify each debit and each credit by the number of the transaction.

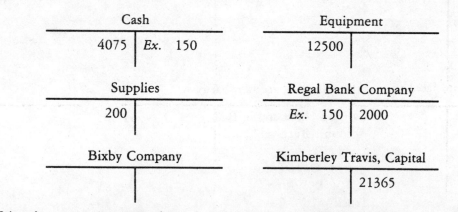

4–4   Using the transactions in Problem 4–3, indicate any increases or decreases in *total* assets, liabilities, and owner's equity.

Trans. No.	Assets	Liabilities	Owner's Equity
Example	Decrease	Decrease	
(1)			
(2)			
(3)			
(4)			

4–5 (1) Open T-accounts for Lori Luing, the owner of Luing's Answering Service, for the following balances, including her owner's equity:

Cash	$ 437.50
Accounts Receivable:	
H. L. Rhodes, MD	50.00
Mary Turner, MD	50.00
T. W. Vine, DDS	35.00
Equipment	2,650.00
Supplies	25.00
Accounts Payable:	
State Telephone Co.	215.00
Ace Electricians	65.00

(2) Complete each of the following transactions, indicating by letter the debits and credits:

a) Received $50, the amount due, from H. L. Rhodes, MD.
b) Paid $65, the amount owed, to Ace Electricians.
c) Bought $75 worth of supplies, paying cash.
d) Invested $500 cash in the business.
e) Received $25 on account from Mary Turner, MD.

(3) Prove that Assets = Liabilities + Owner's Equity.

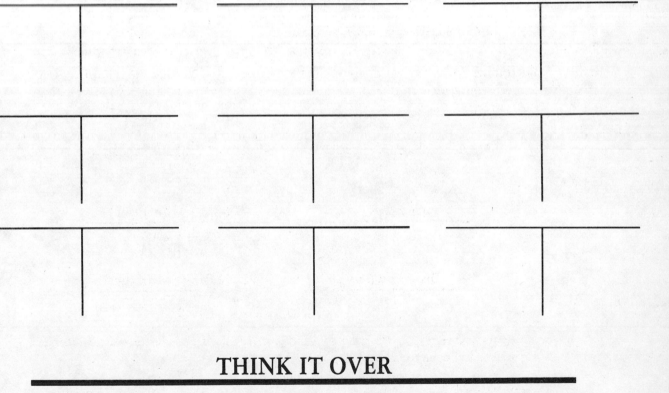

THINK IT OVER

Select any service-type business and consider the many different kinds of transactions that are carried on in any typical day. Think about the reason(s) why the owner is in business. What is his/her goal? What is the "profit motive" that keeps the owner going?

CHAPTER 5

OWNER'S EQUITY ACCOUNTS

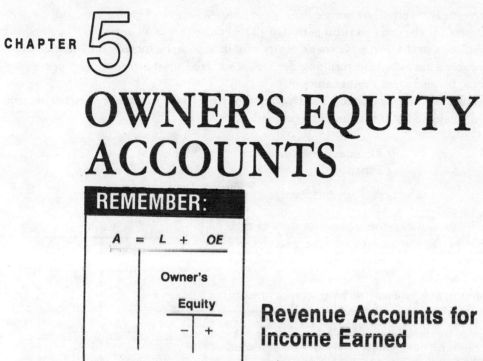

REMEMBER:

$$A = L + OE$$

Owner's

Equity

−	+

Revenue Accounts for Income Earned

A business earns its income (or REVENUE) by selling merchandise and/or services. In this section of this text, all revenue will be earned by charging fees for services performed by the business. The Evergreen Landscaping Service charges each customer a fee for the work performed on a regular basis—weekly or monthly. Special jobs, such as tree removals, are also a source of revenue. The term "revenue" will refer to various fees that are earned by services rendered to the customers of a business. In each case they will be identified by the account title, including the word "income."

Expenses

Any payments made in connection with the earning of revenue are called EXPENSES. These include such items as advertising, rent, employees' salaries, and utilities (heat, light, telephone).

Net Income/Net Loss

If, during a fiscal period, the revenue earned exceeds the total expenses, the business will have a PROFIT or NET INCOME:

Revenue > Total Expenses = Net Income

If, however, expenses exceed revenue, a NET LOSS will result:

$$\boxed{\text{Expenses} > \text{Revenue} = \text{Net Loss}}$$

(In these equations the symbol ">" means "is greater than.")

Effect of Revenue/Expenses on Owner's Equity

Whenever *revenue* is received, owner's equity is *increased*. Whenever *expenses* are paid, owner's equity is *decreased*. At the end of a fiscal period, if all revenue exceeds all expenses, the resulting net income belongs to the owner. Owner's equity will, therefore, be increased by that amount. If expenses exceed revenue, the resulting net loss is suffered by the owner. Owner's equity will, therefore, be decreased by that amount.

Assume that the Evergreen Landscaping Service earned $2,500 in fees last month, and expenses totaled $1,500 for the same period:

Revenue: Fees Income	$2,500
Expenses	1,500
Net Income	$1,000

Revenue and expense transactions will change account balances. The accounts listed on page 26 will change as follows: for the revenue earned (*a*), and for the expenses paid (*b*).

Additional accounts will be opened to record the revenue and expenses. Because *revenue* increases owner's equity, it will be recorded as a *credit*. Because *expenses* decrease owner's equity, they will be recorded as a *debit*. (Expenses are combined in one T-account for this example.)

Cash	
1450	1000
2500	100
5000	(*b*) 1500
(*a*) 2500	

Fees income	
	(*a*) 2500

Expenses	
(*b*) 1500	

By the end of the fiscal period, the fundamental bookkeeping/accounting equation will have changed:

All Assets,	29765	Liabilities,		9045
		Owner's Equity,	19720	
		+ Net Income	1000	20720
Total Assets	29765	= Total Liab. + OE		29765

Owner's Drawing Account

At any time the owner of a business may withdraw cash for personal use, very much like a salary. WITHDRAWALS by the owner, however, are not included with other expenses. Instead, a separate account is opened for the DRAWING ACCOUNT.

Effect of Withdrawal on Owner's Equity

Any *withdrawal* by the owner *decreases owner's equity*; therefore it must be recorded as a *debit*. Note the transaction to record Morales's withdrawal of $500 cash: transaction (*c*).

This transaction changes the fundamental bookkeeping equation: $500 less cash (assets) and $500 less capital (owner's equity).

Cash	
1450	1000
2500	100
5000	1500
2500	(*c*) 500

Thomas Morales, Drawing	
(*c*) 500	

Assets,	29765	Liab.,		9045
−	500	OE,	20720	
		−	500	20220
A	29265	= L	+ OE	29265

Revenue and expenses are temporary owner's equity accounts. They change—increase and decrease—owner's equity. Compare a capital account with revenue and expense accounts:

As *expenses increase* by *debits*, owner's equity decreases.
As *revenue increases* by *credits*, owner's equity increases.

When the owner has made a withdrawal during the fiscal period as well as earned a net income, owner's equity is determined as follows:

Owner's Equity		
Ruth Brown, Capital, October 1,		12 000
Net Income	800	
Less Withdrawals	650	
Net Increase in capital		150
Ruth Brown, Capital, October 31,		12 150

YOU SHOULD REMEMBER

Income *increases owner's equity*; therefore, *income accounts increase by credits*.
Expenses *decrease owner's equity*; therefore, *expense accounts increase by debits*.

KNOW YOUR VOCABULARY

Use each of the following words or terms in a statement relating to bookkeeping/accounting:

Drawing account	Profit
Expenses	Revenue
Net income	Withdrawals
Net loss	

QUESTIONS

1. What are the sources of revenue received by each of the following service businesses?
   a) A tailor
   b) A beauty salon
   c) An architect
   d) A lawyer
   e) A dentist
   f) An accountant
2. What are the typical expenses paid by each of the businesses listed in Question 1?

PROBLEMS

5–1 (1) Open a ledger of T-accounts for Puccio's Taxi Service, owned by Frank Puccio:

Assets:	Cash	$ 562
	Taxis (2)	28,000
	Supplies	150
Liabilities:	Landia National Bank	6,400
	Wilson Garage	75
OE:	Frank Puccio, Capital	?

Open T-accounts for each of these accounts, as well:
  Frank Puccio, Drawing
  Fare Income
  Gas and Oil Expense
  Repairs Expense
  Salary Expense

(2) Record the following transactions, indicating by letter each of the debits and credits:
   a) Collected $250 in fares.
   b) Paid Landia National Bank, $100.
   c) Paid driver's salary, $200.
   d) Withdrew cash for personal use, $300.
   e) Collected $325 in fares.
   f) Paid for gasoline, $45.
   g) Paid Wilson Garage, $75.
   h) Paid for taxi repairs, $40.

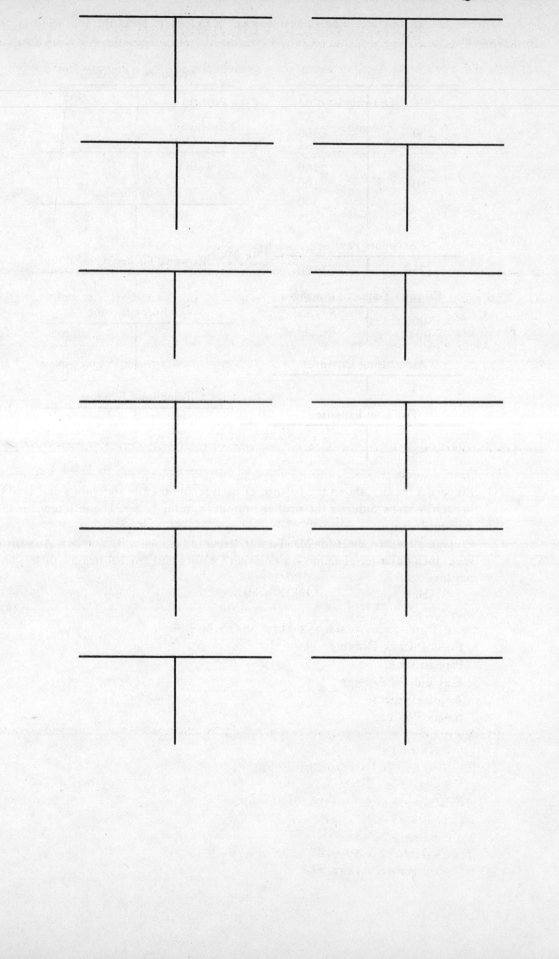

5–2 Rowena Tucker operates a messenger service. Her ledger shows the following information:

Cash		Accounts Receivable	
462	75	875	200
300	75		250
200	300		
600	95		
200	140		
250	100		
	300		
	25		

Delivery Equipment	
12000	

Supplies	
60	
100	

Accounts Payable	
25	1100

Rowena Tucker, Capital	
	12297

Rowena Tucker, Drawing	
300	
300	

Delivery Income	
	300
	600
	200

Advertising Expense	
95	

Telephone Expense	
140	

Trucking Expense	
75	
75	

(1) Prepare a list that shows the balance of each account. (Add the debits and credits in each account. Subtract the smaller amount from the larger. The difference is the account balance.)

(2) Prepare a balance sheet for Ms. Tucker, using today's date. Remember: A balance sheet includes assets, liabilities, and owner's equity plus any net income or less any net loss.

(1) _____

_____

_____

(2) _____

_____

THINK IT OVER

James Lightfoot owns three sporting goods stores, each located in a suburban center near a large midwestern city. For several years he has had a net income. Last year, however, he had a small net loss. He is anxious to find the reason for this loss. Lightfoot maintains one ledger for his business. What would you recommend that he do differently, and why?

CHAPTER **6**

TWO-COLUMN GENERAL JOURNAL

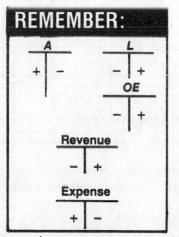

REMEMBER:

Records of business transactions can be entered directly into ledger accounts. However, DIRECT LEDGER bookkeeping can be a difficult and complicated procedure. Since each transaction involves at least one debit equal to one credit, examining one account gives only one half of the information about a transaction. If amounts are similar, finding the other half, even when numbered or lettered, may require a great deal of time. In order to tie together the debits and the credits of the same transaction, every account would have to be examined to find the matching amount.

Bookkeeping/accounting should be orderly. The direct ledger system does not give an orderly running record of all transactions day by day. If an error is made in recording—entering two debits or two credits instead of one of each, or reversing the accounts to be debited and credited, or changing the amount of a debit or credit—locating that error can become a very difficult, time-consuming process. Because there may be hundreds or more entries in a single day, week, or month, the bookkeeping clerk will have to examine each account to find the offsetting amounts in tracing an entry.

Book of Original Entry

To solve this problem, a system of JOURNALS can be used. A journal is a book of ORIGINAL ENTRY, where complete information about a transaction is first recorded. Each page is numbered; columns provide space for a complete date—year, month, day; names of accounts debited and credited; posting references (to be discussed in Chapter 7); and amount columns for debits and for credits. All entries are recorded in CHRONOLOGICAL order as they occur. All information—the date of the transaction, the accounts involved, the amount of each debit and each credit—and any needed explanation are included in this book, a general journal. It becomes the diary of the business for which it is kept.

JOURNAL   Page 12

Date	Account Title	PR	Debit	Credit
198– Sept. 4	Cash		1500 00	
	George Corbo, Capital			1500 00
	Investment			
7	Supplies		100 00	
	Cash			100 00
	Check No. 418			
10	Cash		2000 00	
	Landia National Bank			2000 00
	30-day Loan, Note No. 25			

This general journal illustrates several transactions entered in chronological order on page 12. The first one, dated September 4, is for a $1,500 cash investment made by the owner, George Corbo. The second, dated September 7, is for a $100 cash purchase of supplies. The third, dated September 10, is for a $2,000 cash loan received from the Landia National Bank. Note that zeros are used, rather than a dash, to indicate no cents.

Source Documents

As transactions occur, SOURCE DOCUMENTS are prepared as evidence of these transactions. In some cases the source document may be referred to in the short explanation. A source document is any prepared form or VOUCHER, such as a check or check stub, a numbered bill for services, or a memorandum of a transaction. These will be discussed in more detail in Chapters 14, 15, and 16.

The bookkeeping clerk records additional entries on the next page of the journal, starting again with a complete date:

Date	Account Title	PR	Debit	Credit
198-Sept. 15	Cash		50 00	
	Accounts Receivable (John Smith)		100 00	
	Fees Income			150 00
	Sales Slip No. 284			
20	Equipment		800 00	
	Regional Supply Company			800 00
	Voucher No. 31			

JOURNAL — Page 13

On September 15, services were performed for a customer, John Smith, who was charged $150. We received $50 and he charged the balance, $100. This transaction illustrates a COMPOUND ENTRY, where two accounts are debited and one account is credited. Notice, however, that the debit amounts equal the credit. The other entries illustrated are SIMPLE entries—one debit equal to one credit.

The entry on September 20 is for $800 worth of equipment purchased on account from the Regional Supply Company. This is called a CHARGE purchase, as opposed to a cash purchase. (Accounts Payable could have been credited in this entry; however, it is preferable to show the creditor's balance in an account with an identifiable name.)

Notice that the debit account is always listed first in each journal entry. The account to be credited is indented. The amounts of the debit and credit line up with the account titles. Any explanation is listed below the last account title. The name of the month, with the year, is entered once and is not repeated until the next page. Only the day number is used unless the month changes.

Journalizing

Journalizing *begins with the source document.* The information on it tells the bookkeeping clerk all that is needed for the entry—the date, the names of the accounts to debit and credit, the amount, and, if needed, a brief explanation. Here, for example, is a check stub:

NO. *173* *Oct. 1* 19 *8*			
TO *Ace Realty*			
FOR *Oct. Rent*			
AMOUNT *500.00*			
BAL.	6	253	15
THIS CK.		500	00
BAL.	5	753	15

The entry to record this transaction in a general journal is:

JOURNAL   Page 8

Date	Account Title	PR	Debit	Credit
198– Oct. 1	Rent Expense		500 00	
	Cash			500 00
	Check No. 173			

    Learn the rules of how accounts increase and decrease in order to properly debit and credit accounts. Knowing these rules simplifies the entire journalizing procedure.

YOU SHOULD REMEMBER
Journal entries are listed *chronologically.*
Debit accounts and amounts are always *listed first* in journal entries.
Credit accounts and amounts *are indented following debits.*
A brief explanation ends a journal entry.
In every entry *debits equal credits.*

KNOW YOUR VOCABULARY

Use each of the following words or terms in a statement relating to bookkeeping/accounting:

Book of original entry	Journal
Chronological order	Simple entry
Compound entry	Voucher
Direct ledger	

QUESTIONS

1. If there are 250 transactions in one month, at least how many entries will there probably be in a *ledger* that month?
2. Why would a numbering or lettering system not be practical in recording entries directly in a ledger?
3. Why is a journal similar to a diary?
4. How does the journal entry identify the debit(s) part of any entry compared to the credit part?

PROBLEMS

6–1 Using a general journal, page 7, record each of these transactions for Rose Klein, owner of a dress designing business:

October 2, Paid employee's salary, $175

7, Received $600 cash for a design

14, Paid $200 cash for supplies and material

16, Borrowed $1,000 cash from the Veron Trust Co.

21, Received $500 cash for a design

23, Bought a new $360 drawing table (equipment). Paid $160 cash and charged the balance, $200, to the Textile Equipment Company

30, Withdrew $400 cash for personal use

31, Received $100 cash from Mary Wu, a customer (who bought a design last month for $350 and was charged that amount then)

6–1

		GENERAL JOURNAL				Page 7	
Date		Account Title	PR	Debit		Credit	
Oct	2	Salary Expense		175 —			
		Cash				175 —	
		Employees Salary					
	7	Cash		600 —			
		Design Income				600 —	
		Received for a design					

6–2   What would be a typical source document for each of the transactions listed in Problem 6–1?

THINK IT OVER

Simon Bredhoff has been using the direct ledger method in his bookkeeping records. His business activity has been increasing in recent months. Exactly what should Bredhoff do in order to maintain better control, giving him a more immediate and continuous set of information, and allowing him to follow his business activities day by day?

Ethel Cosmos keeps a ledger and a general journal for her professional consulting business. As each transaction occurs, she wonders which would be the wiser action:

(1)   to enter debits and credits in accounts to keep account balances up to date, or

(2)   to journalize each transaction first, to keep a running record.

What help can you offer Cosmos in making a decision that will help her follow her business in a more logical way? Which logically comes first: the journal or the ledger?

CHAPTER 7

POSTING THE GENERAL JOURNAL

The system of recording transactions in a general journal does not replace the use of ledger accounts. At some point, each *amount* debited or credited in the journal must be transferred to the ledger account named in the journal entry. This step is called POSTING. Posting should be done on a regular—daily, weekly, or monthly—basis, depending on the frequency of transactions.

Posting Procedure

Every ledger account must be numbered. Each one appears on a separate page or card with a number that identifies the type of account:

Classification	Account Number
Assets	11–19
Liabilities	21–29
Owner's Equity	31–39
Revenue	41–49
Expenses	51–59

If more accounts are needed in any classification, the entire ledger must be renumbered in the hundreds: 111–199; 211–299; 311–399; 411–499; 511–599.

JOURNAL TO LEDGER

The steps in posting a journal entry are as follows:

(1) Enter, for the account debited, the *amount* on the debit side of that account: · — · — (see illustration below).

(2) Enter the date—year, month, and day (thereafter, do not repeat the year and month): — — — .

(3) Enter the *journal* page number in the Posting Reference (PR) column of the account: ·-·-·-·-·-·-· .

(4) Enter the *account number* in the Posting Reference (PR) column of the journal:■-■-■-■-■ .

Repeat the posting procedure for the next account listed in the journal. Continue with each journal entry, posting debits and credits to each of the accounts listed. If the work of posting is interrupted, the bookkeeping clerk will always know exactly where to resume work—after the last posting reference *account number* in the journal PR column.

Just as debits must equal credits in each journal entry, debits must equal credits when posted to ledger accounts. The following journal entry will be posted to the accounts involved. (Assume that cash has an $800 debit balance (√) from the preceding month.)

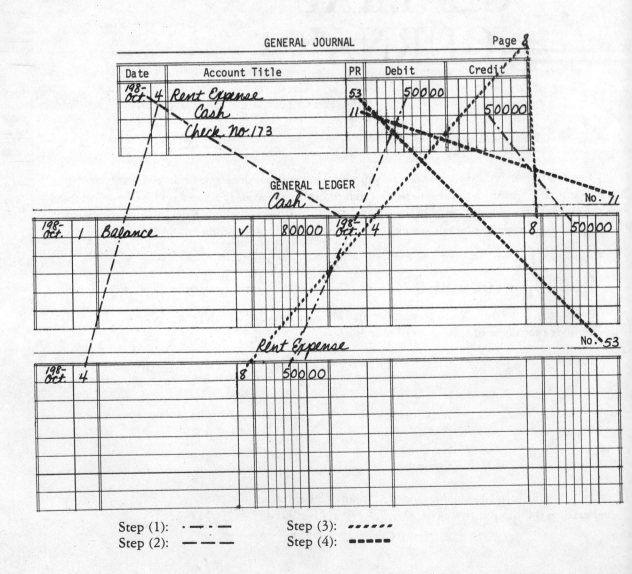

| Step (1): · — · — | Step (3): ·-·-·-· |
| Step (2): — — — | Step (4): ■-■-■-■ |

CROSS REFERENCING

It is now possible to tie together quickly the debit and credit for each transaction. Posting references refer to each other—the journal to the account number, the account to the journal page number. This is called CROSS REFERENCING. It makes the work of checking the records much simpler.

The bookkeeping process starts with the source document for a transaction. A journal entry is then recorded. The entry is posted to ledger accounts:

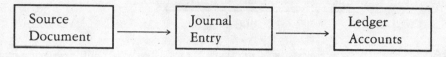

Trial Balance

When all journalizing and posting have been completed at the end of a fiscal period, or at the end of a month, the bookkeeping clerk makes a check on the accuracy of that work. A listing is made of all ledger accounts and their balances; this is called a TRIAL BALANCE.

In preparing a trial balance, the following steps are taken:

(1) Find the balance of each account, using pencil. Total all debits and credits; these are written below the last figure on each side. This is called FOOTING the ledger, and the totals are called *pencil footings.*

(2) Subtract the smaller footing from the larger (on scrap paper). In pencil, write the difference, or BALANCE of the account, on the *larger side* in the item column. Accounts will normally have balances (debit or credit) on their *increase* sides—assets are debits, liabilities are credits, owner's equity (capital) is a credit, revenue is a credit, and expenses are debits.

								Supplies			No. *16*
198- Oct.	2		3		100 00	198- Oct.	28		9		20 00
	14		7		50 00						
	30		10		35 00						
		165.00			185 00						

Above is a typical account that has pencil footings and a balance. Since only one credit is posted, there is no need to total that side of the account. This account, an asset, has a debit balance of $165.00.

(3) Start the trial balance with a heading to answer the questions WHO, WHAT, and WHEN.

(4) List all accounts by name in their numerical order. Each account balance is placed in either the first (debit) or second (credit) money column (see page 48).

(5) Finally, total each column. If all work is done correctly, the totals should be equal. Once again debits equal credits. The trial balance is said to be IN BALANCE. Double-rule the totals to show that the work has been completed.

Following is a ledger of simple T-account balances:

Cash	Equipment	Supplies
2500		5000		300	

Accounts Payable	De Van Loc, Capital	Rent Income
	1200		5150		2000

Advertising Expense	Salary Expense
150		400	

At the end of the fiscal period (October 31) the bookkeeping clerk will prepare a trial balance of the general ledger, following the five steps listed above.

De Van Loc Company
Trial Balance
October 31, 198—

Account Title	Acct. No.	Debit	Credit
Cash		2500 00	
Equipment		5000 00	
Supplies		300 00	
Accounts Payable			1200 00
De Van Loc, Capital			5150 00
Rent Income			2000 00
Advertising Expense		150 00	
Salary Expense		400 00	
		8350 00	8350 00

YOU SHOULD REMEMBER

Account *balances* normally appear on the debit or credit side on which *the account increases.*
A trial balance *proves* the *equality of debits and credits in the ledger.*

KNOW YOUR VOCABULARY

Balance	In balance
Cross referencing	Posting
Footings	Trial balance

QUESTIONS

1. What steps are followed in posting journal entries?
2. On which side of accounts are balances normally found?
3. a) What does the journal posting refer to?
   b) What does the account posting refer to?
4. A bookkeeping clerk resumes his/her posting work after returning from lunch. How will he/she know where to resume?
5. What does a trial balance "in balance" prove?

PROBLEMS

7–1   Post from the general journal to the ledger accounts the following entries:

GENERAL JOURNAL   Page 6

198-					
Oct.	1	Equipment	1000 00		
		Landers Mfg. Co.		1000 00	
		5 Motors, Voucher No. 31			
	10	Cash	2500 00		
		Service Income		2500 00	
		Receipts Nos. 1-35, to date			
	18	L. D. Berger, Drawing	500 00		
		Cash		500 00	
		Withdrawal, Personal Use,			
		Check No. 57			
	25	Landers Mfg. Company	250 00		
		Cash		250 00	
		Partial Payment, Check No. 58			

(A partial ledger is shown here.)

Cash   No. 11

198– Oct.	1	Balance	√	1750 00			

Equipment   No. 12

198– Oct.	1	Balance	√	3000 00			

Landers Mfg. Company   No. 21

L. D. Berger, Drawing   No. 32

Service Income   41

7-2 Below, in T-account form, is the general ledger for Harold Kriss, who operates a computer consulting firm:

Cash			No. 11
1500 00		100	00
750 00		50	00
495 00		75	00
2745		500	00

2020

Hi-Tech Company		No. 21
75 00		2000 00

725

Harold Kriss, Capital		No. 31
		3060 00

Services Income		No. 41
		750 00
		495 00

Equipment		No. 12
3500 00		
465 00		

Supplies		No. 13
60 00		

Comp-Software Company		No. 22
		465 00

Harold Kriss, Drawing		No. 32
500 00		

Advertising Expense		No. 51
100 00		

Utilities Expense		No. 52
50 00		

(1) Pencil-foot the ledger to find the balance of each account.
(2) Prepare a trial balance, using today's date.

Harold Kriss
Trial Balance
06-28-95

			Debit		Credit	
Cash	11		2020	—		
Equipment	12		3965	—		
Supplies	13		60	—		
Hi Ted Co.	21				1925	—
Comp Software Co	22				465	—
Harold Kriss Capital	31				3060	—
Harold Kriss Drawing	32		500	—		
Service Income	41				1245	—
Advertising Expense	51		100	—		
Utilities Expense	52		50	—		
			6695	—	6695	—

7–3   Anita Schaffer runs knitting and sewing classes from her home. Last month she completed the following transactions:

October 2,   Bought class supplies for cash, $125
      7,   Received class fees, $200
    11,   Made a $50 payment to Jessup Bank due on loan
    21,   Received class fees, $240
    27,   Paid $65 for miscellaneous expenses
    31,   Withdrew for personal use, $300

(1)   Record the transactions above in Schaffer's journal.
(2)   Post the journal entries to Schaffer's ledger accounts.
(3)   Foot the ledger accounts, indicating the balances at the end of the month.
(4)   Prepare a trial balance, dated October 31, 198–.

(1)   GENERAL JOURNAL   Page 3

Date	Account Title	PR	Debit	Credit

(2) and (3)

Cash   No. 11

Date		Item	PR	Debit	Date	Item	PR	Credit
198– Oct.	1	Balance	✓	1375 00				

Equipment   No. 12

Date		Item	PR	Debit	Date	Item	PR	Credit
198– Oct.	1	Balance	✓	1642 50				

Supplies   No. 13

Date		Item	PR	Debit	Date	Item	PR	Credit
198– Oct.	1	Balance	✓	230 00				

Jessup Bank   No. 21

Date	Item	PR	Debit	Date		Item	PR	Credit
				198– Oct.	1	Balance	✓	875 00

Anita Schaffer, Capital   No. 31

Date	Item	PR	Debit	Date		Item	PR	Credit
				198– Oct.	1	Balance	✓	2372 50

Anita Schaffer, Drawing   No. 32

Date	Item	PR	Debit	Date	Item	PR	Credit

Fee Income   No. 41

Date	Item	PR	Debit	Date	Item	PR	Credit

Miscellaneous Expense   No. 51

Date	Item	PR	Debit	Date	Item	PR	Credit

(4)

THINK IT OVER

Dina Fowler has prepared a trial balance for her business. It is not in balance. She asks you where she should review her bookkeeping work, in order to find the reason. What suggestions will you make?

Ira Jacobs has prepared a trial balance that is in balance. On reviewing one entry, however, he discovers that he omitted another entry for a payment of $50 for an expense. Why did this error, or omission, not affect the equality of debits and credits in his ledger?

Can you suggest any other kinds of errors that might not cause a trial balance to be "out of balance"?

CHAPTER 8

THE TRIAL BALANCE AND WORK SHEET

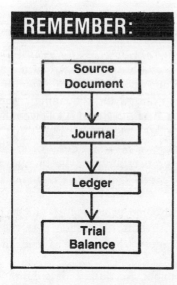

REMEMBER:

Source Document → Journal → Ledger → Trial Balance

Locating Errors

A trial balance taken at the time interval desired—end of month, fiscal period, year—is a test of the equality of the debit and credit balances in the ledger. If, however, a trial balance is OUT OF BALANCE, the following steps—in reverse order—should be taken to determine the reason(s):

(1) Re-add the columns of the trial balance; perhaps they were totaled incorrectly.

(2) Examine each account balance in the trial balance, and compare these account balances to the ledger account balances. Perhaps they were carried forward incorrectly, or perhaps an account was omitted, listed twice, or placed in the wrong amount column of the trial balance (reversing a debit and a credit).

(3) Re-foot the ledger accounts to verify each account balance.

(4) If an error is not located at this point, compare each entry in the account with the original debit and credit recorded in the journal entry.

When an error is discovered in the ledger, neatly cross out the incorrect entry and write the correction above it. Never erase ink amounts or mark through an error in any way that causes the first figure to be altered. This could cause legal problems, inasmuch as book-keeping/accounting records are legal documents.

Errors That the Trial Balance Does Not Reveal

Not all errors show up in a trial balance. The following errors do not affect the equality of debits and credits in the ledger:

(1) Omitting an entire entry.
(2) Posting to an incorrect account—a debit to another debit, a credit to another credit.
(3) Using an incorrect amount in a journal entry and posting that amount to ledger accounts.
(4) Recording a transaction twice.

The Six-Column Work Sheet

By the end of a fiscal period, the owner of a business wants the answer to a very important question: What was the net income or net loss for that period? To answer that question, a WORK SHEET is prepared. A work sheet is a ruled form of analysis paper with several columns. Because it is not part of the permanent records, however, it can be completed in pencil. The steps taken to complete a work sheet are as follows:

(1) Write a heading that answers the questions WHO, WHAT, and WHEN. The "when" part indicates the fiscal period *ending date.*
(2) List all ledger accounts and their balances in the first pair of money columns, arranged as they would be in a trial balance.
(3) Extend the balance of each account to one of the remaining columns by determining whether the account is a BALANCE SHEET account—assets, liabilities, and owner's equity—and a debit or credit, or an INCOME STATEMENT account—revenue, expenses—and a debit or credit.
(4) Total all remaining columns; the difference between the Income Statement columns and the difference between the Balance Sheet columns should be equal.
(5) Determine whether there was a net income or a net loss. In the Income Statement *column totals*, if the credit (revenue) is greater than the debit (expenses), there has been a net income; if the reverse is true, there has been a net loss.
(6) Identify the net income or net loss in the Account Title column; the amount is entered in the smaller of the two Income Statement and Balance Sheet columns; equal totals are then entered in each pair of columns and they are double ruled.

Examine carefully the completed work sheet on page 57. It begins with the trial balance completed for the De Van Loc Company, illustrated in Chapter 7, page 48. Note the heading (1), the trial balance (2), extending the account balances (3), totaling the last four columns and finding the difference (4), determining the amount of net income (5), and adding it to the lesser amount in both the income statement and balance sheet totals to make them equal, then double ruling (6).

De Van Loc Company
Work Sheet
For the Month Ended October 31, 198-

Account Title	A. N.	Trial Balance Debit	Trial Balance Credit	Income Statement Debit	Income Statement Credit	Balance Sheet Debit	Balance Sheet Credit
Cash	11	250000				250000	
Equipment	12	500000				500000	
Supplies	13	30000				30000	
Accounts Payable	21		120000				120000
De Van Loc, Capital	31		515000				515000
Rent Income	41		200000		200000		
Advertising Expense	51	15000		15000			
Salary Expense	52	40000		40000			
		835000	835000	55000	200000	780000	635000
Net Income				145000			145000
				200000	200000	780000	780000

KNOW YOUR VOCABULARY

Balance sheet	Net loss
Income statement	Out of balance
Net income	Work sheet

QUESTIONS

1. What is the order in which work will be checked to find an error in the trial balance?
2. What errors will cause a trial balance to be out of balance?
3. What errors can be made that will not cause a trial balance to be out of balance?
4. How is the net income or net loss for the fiscal period determined on the work sheet?

PROBLEMS

8–1 T. R. Price is a carpenter who receives a commission for odd jobs in his neighborhood. His bookkeeping records indicate the following balances (shown in T-account form):

Cash	Equipment	Truck
2645	1500	7500

County Mfg. Co.	T. R. Price, Capital	T. R. Price, Drawing
550	10570	500

Commissions Income	Advertising Expense	Miscellaneous Expense
1650	100	50

Rent Expense	Salary Expense
175	300

Complete a six-column work sheet for the month ended November 30, 198–. (Save your work for future problems.)

Account Title	A. N.	Trial Balance Debit	Trial Balance Credit	Income Statement Debit	Income Statement Credit	Balance Sheet Debit	Balance Sheet Credit
Cash		2645				2645	
Equipment		1500				1500	
Truck		7500				7500	
County Mfg.			550				550
T R Price Capital			10570				10570
T Price Drawing		500				500	
Commissions Income			1650		1650		
Advertising Expense		100		100			
Misc Expense		50		50			
Rent Expense		175		175			
Salary Expense		300		300			
		12770	12770	625	1650	12145	11120
				1025			1025
				1650	1650	12145	12145

8-2 Below is a trial balance for Ann Danziger; however, it contains an error.

Danziger Designs
Trial Balance
September 30, 198-

Cash	176250	176250
Accounts Receivable	73890	
Equipment	260500	
Supplies	39500	
Accounts Payable	60000	
Ann Danziger, Capital		425140
Ann Danziger, Drawing	80000	
Fees Income		240000
Advertising Expense	16000	
Insurance Expense	4000	
Materials Expense	10000	
Rent Expense	25000	
Salary Expense	40000	

(1) Find the error, correcting the trial balance.

(2)   Complete the work sheet for the quarter year ended September 30. (Save your work for future problems.)

Account Title	A. N.	Trial Balance		Income Statement		Balance Sheet	
		Debit	Credit	Debit	Credit	Debit	Credit

8–3   Rebecca Gayle operates a message delivery service. Her trial balance for the month ended October 31, 198–, is shown below:

Gayle's Reliable Service
Trial Balance
October 31, 198–

Cash	760 00	
Accounts Receivable	142 50	
Automobile	9200 00	
Supplies	350 00	
County Bank & Trust Co.		360 00
Rebecca Gayle, Capital		6302 00
Rebecca Gayle, Drawing	600 00	
Service Income		1875 50
Advertising Expense	200 00	
Auto Expense	400 00	
Miscellaneous Expense	60 00	
Telephone Expense	75 00	

(1)   Total the trial balance.

(2)   Complete the work sheet. (Save your work for future problems.)

Account Title	A. N.	Trial Balance		Income Statement		Balance Sheet	
		Debit	Credit	Debit	Credit	Debit	Credit

THINK IT OVER

Damien Spyridon's trial balance is not in balance. He checks his work and finds two errors. An expense account with a $100 balance was listed on the trial balance as a credit. The other error is found when he checks his posting. A journal entry amount was $54; he posted the debit as $45. Why did the trial balance columns differ by $209?

CHAPTER **9**

FINANCIAL STATEMENTS

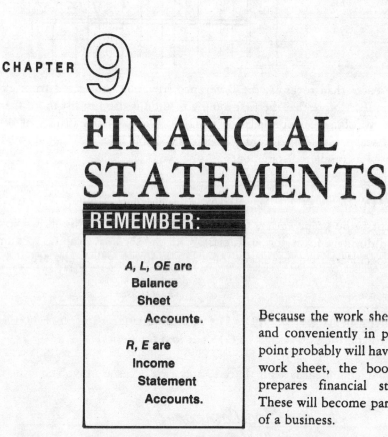

REMEMBER:

A, L, OE are
Balance
Sheet
    Accounts.

R, E are
Income
Statement
    Accounts.

Because the work sheet can be completed easily and conveniently in pencil, all errors up to that point probably will have been corrected. Using the work sheet, the bookkeeping/accounting clerk prepares financial statements more formally. These will become part of the permanent records of a business.

Income Statement—Form and Content

An INCOME STATEMENT is prepared first, using the information in the Income Statement columns of the work sheet. The heading will answer the questions WHO, WHAT, and WHEN. All revenue is listed first, and totaled. Expenses are then listed, totaled, and subtracted from total revenue. The difference is the same net income (or net loss) as shown on the work sheet.

Revenue − Expenses = Net Income or Net Loss

Follow this illustration (based on the work sheet on page 57).

De Van Loc Company
Income Statement
For the Month Ended October 31, 198-

Revenue:			
Rent Income			2000 00
Expenses:			
Advertising Expense		1 50 00	
Salary Expense		4 00 00	
Total Expenses			5 50 00
Net Income			1 450 00

If expenses are greater than revenue, the difference (revenue subtracted from expenses) is identified as a net loss. Note that the first money column is used to list more than one item; the second money column is for totals (or a single item) and the results of the business operations for the fiscal period—net income or net loss. Double lines are ruled through both money columns to show a completed statement.

Capital Statement

The next financial statement to be prepared is a CAPITAL STATEMENT. This shows how owner's equity has changed during a fiscal period. It starts with the *beginning* capital account balance. Any changes that occur are then listed. Possible changes in owner's equity are:

Increases	Decreases
(1) additional investments	(1) withdrawals
(2) net income for period	(2) net loss for period

De Van Loc's capital statement is a simple one; only two items are involved.

De Van Loc Company
Capital Statement
For the Month Ended October 31, 198-

Beginning Balance, Oct. 1, 198-			5 150 00
Plus: Net Income			1 450 00
Ending Balance, Oct. 31, 198-			6 600 00

Following are illustrations of capital statements with more changes (headings are omitted here):

Beginning Balance, Sept. 1, 198–		7500 00
Plus: Additional Investment	1000 00	
Net Income	2500 00	
	3500 00	
Less: Withdrawals	1500 00	
Net Increase in Capital		2000 00
Ending Balance, Sept. 30, 198–		9500 00

With decreases less than increases, there is a *net increase* in capital. Always verify whichever one there is before writing the words "Net Increase" or "Net Decrease."

Beginning Balance, Nov. 1, 198–			12500 00
Plus: Additional Investment		3000 00	
Less: Withdrawals	1500 00		
Net Loss	2000 00	3500 00	
Net Decrease in Capital			500 00
Ending Balance, Nov. 30, 198–			12000 00

Balance Sheet—Form and Content

The next financial statement to be prepared is one that was discussed in Chapter 3—a balance sheet. The information is found in the Balance Sheet columns of the work sheet, *except for owner's equity*. The capital *at the end of the fiscal period* is the ending balance found on the capital statement.

De Van Loc Company Balance Sheet October 31, 198—					
Assets			**Liabilities**		
Cash	2500	00	Accounts Payable	1200	00
Equipment	5000	00	Owner's Equity		
Supplies	300	00	De Van Loc, Cap, Oct. 31	6600	00
Total Assets	7800	00	Total Liab. + O.E.	7800	00

Compare De Van Loc's capital with the amount listed on his capital statement, page 64. These two items will always agree.

YOU SHOULD REMEMBER

When *revenue is greater than expenses* there is a *net income*.
When *expenses are greater than revenue* there is a net loss.
Owner's equity is *increased* by:
   —additional investments and
   —net income.
Owner's equity is *decreased* by:
   —withdrawals by the owner and
   —net loss.

KNOW YOUR VOCABULARY

Balance sheet   Income statement
Capital statement

QUESTIONS

1. From which source of information are financial statements prepared?
2. In what order should statements be prepared?
3. What are the causes for an increase in owner's equity?
4. What are the causes for a decrease in owner's equity?
5. Why is the work sheet capital balance not used in completing a balance sheet?
6. How are the dates indicated in the "when" part of each statement's heading?

PROBLEMS

9–1 Using the completed work sheet in Problem 8–1 for T. R. Price, complete the following:
   a) An income statement.
   b) A capital statement.
   c) A balance sheet.

a)

b)

c)

9–2 Using the completed work sheet in Problem 8–2 for Danziger Designs, complete the following:

    a) An income statement.
    b) A capital statement.
    c) A balance sheet.

a)

b)

c)

9–3 Using the completed work sheet in Problem 8–3 for Rebecca Gayle, complete the following:

    a) An income statement.
    b) A capital statement.
    c) A balance sheet.

a)

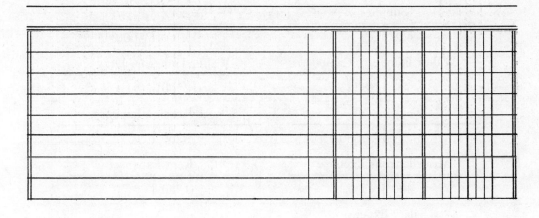

b)

c)

9–4 Below is the T-account ledger for Walter Finnegan Associates, an architectural consulting firm:

Cash	Accounts Receivable
5648		2655	

Equipment	Truck
10400		15000	

Supplies	Accounts Payable
420			8600

Walter Finnegan, Capital	Walter Finnegan, Drawing
	28243	2500	

Fees Income	Advertising Expense
	3680	800	

Miscellaneous Expense	Rent Expense
400		1200	

Salary Expense	
1500		

(1) Complete a work sheet for the month ended November 30, 198–.
(2) Complete the following:
 a) An income statement.
 b) A capital statement. Assume that Finnegan's beginning capital was $25,243, and an additional $3,000 was invested during the fiscal period.
 c) A balance sheet.

(1)

Account Title	A. N.	Trial Balance		Income Statement		Balance Sheet	
		Debit	Credit	Debit	Credit	Debit	Credit

2a) _____

2b) _____

2c) _____

THINK IT OVER

A balance sheet has been compared to a photograph. An income statement has been compared to a moving picture. What might be the explanation for such comparisons?

CHAPTER 10

CLOSING THE LEDGER

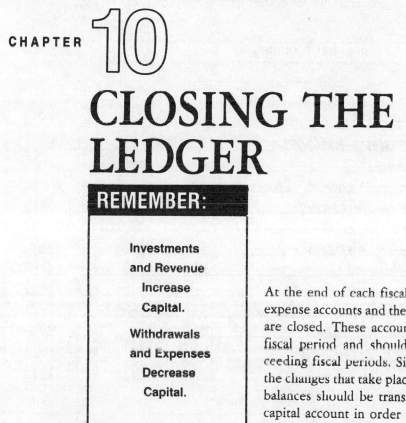

REMEMBER:

Investments and Revenue Increase Capital.

Withdrawals and Expenses Decrease Capital.

At the end of each fiscal period, all revenue and expense accounts and the owner's drawing account are closed. These accounts list information for a fiscal period and should not carry over to succeeding fiscal periods. Since these accounts show the changes that take place in owner's equity, their balances should be transferred to the permanent capital account in order to bring that account up to date. After being closed, these accounts can be used again, starting at a zero balance, for recording revenue, expenses, and withdrawals for the next fiscal period.

Revenue and Expense Summary

To close an account, an entry must be made which will result in posting on the opposite side of that account an amount equal to its balance. The CLOSING ENTRY procedure will reduce the balance of all revenue, expense, and drawing accounts to zero.

Revenue accounts are closed first. Since they have credit balances, they must be debited in order to have zero balances. The account credited is REVENUE AND EXPENSE SUMMARY, an owner's equity account used for special entries, including this closing procedure. This account is used to summarize the changes caused by income and expenses each fiscal period.

The second closing entry will ZERO OUT expense accounts. Since they have debit balances, they must be credited in order to have zero balances. The account debited is Revenue and Expense Summary.

The third closing entry will zero out the balance of the Revenue and Expense Summary account. The amount will always be equal to the *net income* or *net loss* for the fiscal period. If there is a net income, the summary account has a credit balance; if there is a net loss, the summary account has a debit balance. This closing entry *increases capital* for the amount of the *net income*, or *decreases capital* for the amount of the *net loss*, whichever has occurred during the fiscal period.

The following are the closing entries for the De Van Loc Company (see work sheet, page 57, Income Statement columns). These entries have been posted to the ledger accounts affected.

GENERAL JOURNAL   Page 4

Date	Account Title	PR	Debit	Credit
	Closing Entries			
198– Oct. 31	Rent Income	41	2000 00	
	Revenue and Expense Summary	33		2000 00
	to close income acct.			
31	Revenue and Expense Summary	33	550 00	
	Advertising Expense	51		150 00
	Salary Expense	52		400 00
	to close expense accts.			
31	Revenue and Expense Summary	33	1450 00	
	De Van Loc, Capital	31		1450 00
	to close net income			

LEDGER

De Van Loc, Capital   No. 31

					198– Oct.	1	Balance	✓	5150 00
						31		4	1450 00

Revenue and Expense Summary   No. 33

198– Oct.	31		4	550 00	198– Oct.	31		4	2000 00
	31		4	1450 00					

Rent Income
No. 41

198– Oct.	31		4	2000 00	198– Oct.	15		2	1000 00
						30		3	1000 00
									2000 00

Advertising Expense
No. 51

198– Oct.	5		1	150 00	198– Oct.	31		4	150 00

Salary Expense
No. 52

198– Oct.	7		1	100 00	198– Oct.	31		4	400 00
	14		2	100 00					
	21		2	100 00					
	28		3	100 00					
				400 00					

A fourth closing entry is needed if the owner has made withdrawals during the fiscal period. Assume that John Wade's capital balance on November 30 is $12,750. His drawing account indicates withdrawals of $1,200. His net loss for the fiscal period is $500. The following are his third and fourth closing entries, which have been posted to the accounts affected.

GENERAL JOURNAL
Page 8

198– Nov.	30	John Wade, Capital	31		500 00	
		Revenue and Expense Summary	33			500 00
		to close net loss				
	30	John Wade, Capital	31		1200 00	
		John Wade, Drawing	32			1200 00
		to close withdrawals				

LEDGER

John Wade, Capital   No. 31

198- Nov.	30		8	500 00	198- Nov.	1	Balance	✓	1750 00
	30		8	1200 00					
							(Closing Entry No. 3)		
							(Closing Entry No. 4)		

John Wade, Drawing   No. 32

198- Nov.	15		6	600 00	198- Nov.	30		8	1200 00
	30		7	600 00					
							(Closing Entry No. 4)		

Revenue and Expense Summary   No. 33

198- Nov.	30		8	3000 00	198- Nov.	30		8	2500 00
						30		8	500 00
							(Closing Entry No. 3)		

Accounts Closed/Accounts Open—Ruling, Balancing

Accounts that are closed have zero balances—all revenue, expenses, the summary account, and the drawing account. To show this clearly, they are totaled on both sides and ruled with double lines. An account that is closed and ruled is illustrated as follows.

Salary Expense   No. 517

198- Dec.	20		19	300 00	198- Dec.	31		22	600 00
	30		21	300 00					
				600 00					600 00

All ledger accounts, starting with the drawing account, would be ruled in this way. They have no balances; they are closed at the end of the fiscal period.

Balance sheet accounts, on the other hand, have balances that carry over to the next fiscal period. These accounts are BALANCED AND RULED. The following steps are taken:

(1) Pencil-foot the ledger—already done to take a trial balance; see page 47, steps (1) and (2).

(2) Enter in ink on the *smaller side* the amount of the account balance (√) so that both sides are equal.

(3) Write total amounts on the same line level on both debit and credit sides; double-rule the account through the date and money columns.

(4) Enter the account balance on the *larger side* as of the first day of the next fiscal period, with the word "Balance" and check mark (√) in the posting reference column.

The following are two typical accounts that have been balanced and ruled.

Cash   No. 111

198–						198–					
Dec.	1	Balance	√	1520 00		Dec.	20		19	300 00	
	15		17	390 00			30		21	300 00	
	30		21	860 00			31	Balance	√	2170 00	
		2170.00			2770 00					2770 00	
198– Jan.	1	Balance	√	2170 00							

Eleanor Smith, Capital   No. 311

198–						198–					
Dec.	31		22	800 00		Dec.	1	Balance	√	15000 00	
	31	Balance	√	16200 00			31		22	2000 00	
					17000 00			16200.00		17000 00	
						198– Jan.	1	Balance	√	16200 00	

If an account has entries on one side only, it does not have to be formally balanced and ruled. Either the pencil footing or the single-entry amount stands out clearly as the balance.

Supplies   No. 115

198–										
Dec.	5		14	35 00						
	19		16	110 00						
				145 00						

To prove the equality of ledger debits and credits after the balancing and ruling procedure, the bookkeeping/accounting clerk prepares another trial balance—a POST-CLOSING TRIAL BALANCE. All debit account balances must equal all credit account balances. These accounts will list the same balances that are reported on the balance sheet. However, the capital account will now be updated for any net increases or net decreases that may have occurred during the fiscal period.

Compare the post-closing trial balance for De Van Loc Company with the trial balance prepared earlier (see page 48).

De Van Loc Company
Post-closing Trial Balance
October 31, 198—

	Debit	Credit
Cash	2500 00	
Equipment	5000 00	
Supplies	300 00	
Accounts Payable		1200 00
De Van Loc, Capital		6600 00
	7800 00	7800 00

A complete BOOKKEEPING/ACCOUNTING CYCLE has been illustrated in the work done to date. To complete such a cycle follow these steps carefully:

(1) Journalize transactions.
(2) Post to ledger accounts.
(3) Prepare a trial balance.
(4) Prepare a work sheet and financial statements.
(5) Make closing entries and post to accounts.
(6) Balance and rule ledger.
(7) Prepare the post-closing trial balance.

YOU SHOULD REMEMBER

The Revenue and Expense Summary account is used in closing entries *to zero out revenue and expense account balances*.

The *balance of the Revenue and Expense Summary Account* after zeroing out revenue and expense account balances *equals the net income or net loss* for the fiscal period.

After all closing entries are posted, *the Capital account* balance *equals* the amount of *owner's equity* as indicated on the capital statement and the balance sheet

---

KNOW YOUR VOCABULARY

Balance and rule

Bookkeeping/accounting cycle

Closing entry

Post-closing trial balance

Revenue and expense summary

Zero out

QUESTIONS

1. How are net increases and/or decreases transferred to the owner's capital account?
2. What are the four closing entries in correct order?
3. What does a credit balance in the Revenue and Expense Summary account represent?
4. What closing entry is made when the Revenue and Expense Summary account has a debit balance?
5. How is a revenue account closed?
6. How are expense accounts and the drawing account closed?
7. Which accounts remain open at the end of each fiscal period?

PROBLEMS

10–1 The following is the *partial work sheet* for Gwen Vreeland, a publishers' consultant and editor. Journalize her four closing entries at the end of the annual fiscal period *after determining the amount of her net income or net loss*. (Note that her withdrawals for the period were $1,800. This would appear in the Balance Sheet column of the work sheet.) Explanations are not needed for these entries, inasmuch as the words "Closing Entries" are written before the first one is recorded.

Account Title	A. N.	Trial Balance Debit	Trial Balance Credit	Income Statement Debit	Income Statement Credit
Cash		2000 00			
Furniture and Fixtures		5000 00			
Supplies		350 00			
Accounts Payable			1000 00		
Gwen Vreeland, Capital			4800 00		
Gwen Vreeland, Drawing		1800 00			
Consulting Fees Income			3750 00		3750 00
Royalty Income			500 00		500 00
Advertising Expense		100 00		100 00	
Miscellaneous Expense		60 00		60 00	
Rent Expense		250 00		250 00	
Salary Expense		400 00		400 00	
Telephone Expense		90 00		90 00	
		10050 00	10050 00	900 00	4250 00

10–2   Below is a listing of the ledger accounts and their balances for the Allen Insurance Agency.

Cash	$ 800.00
Accounts Receivable	3,895.00
Equipment	4,000.00
Automobile	12,500.00
Supplies	750.00
Accounts Payable	6,000.00
Elliot Allen, Capital	12,920.00
Elliot Allen, Drawing	1,500.00
Commissions Income	6,500.00
Automobile Expense	600.00
Office Expense	175.00
Rent Expense	300.00
Salary Expense	900.00

(1)   Complete a work sheet for the month ended November 30, 198–.

(2)   Journalize the four closing entries.

(1)

Account Title	A. N.	Trial Balance Debit	Credit	Income Statement Debit	Credit	Balance Sheet Debit	Credit

(2)

10–3   Earl Alpert, an attorney, has asked you to complete the work indicated:

(1)   Complete the work sheet below.

Earl Alpert, Esquire
Work Sheet
For 3 Months Ended June 30, 198—

Account Title	A.N.	Trial Balance Debit	Trial Balance Credit	Income Statement Debit	Income Statement Credit	Balance Sheet Debit	Balance Sheet Credit
Cash	11	1 605 00					
Accounts Receivable	12	1 458 00					
Office Equipment	13	396 00					
Furniture	14	525 00					
Supplies	15	830 75					
Accounts Payable	21		1 875 00				
Earl Alpert, Capital	31		24 300 75				
Earl Alpert, Drawing	32	4 800 00					
Legal Fees Income	41		9 500 00				
Miscellaneous Expense	51	150 00					
Office Expense	52	225 00					
Rent Expense	53	1 200 00					
Salary Expense	54	3 000 00					
Travel Expense	55	75 00					

(2)   Complete the following financial statements:

a)   An income statement.

b)   A capital statement. Assume that Alpert's capital was $23,300.75 at the beginning of the fiscal period; he made an additional investment of $1,000 during the fiscal period.

c)   A balance sheet.

(3)   Journalize the closing entries.

2a)

2b)

2c)

(3)

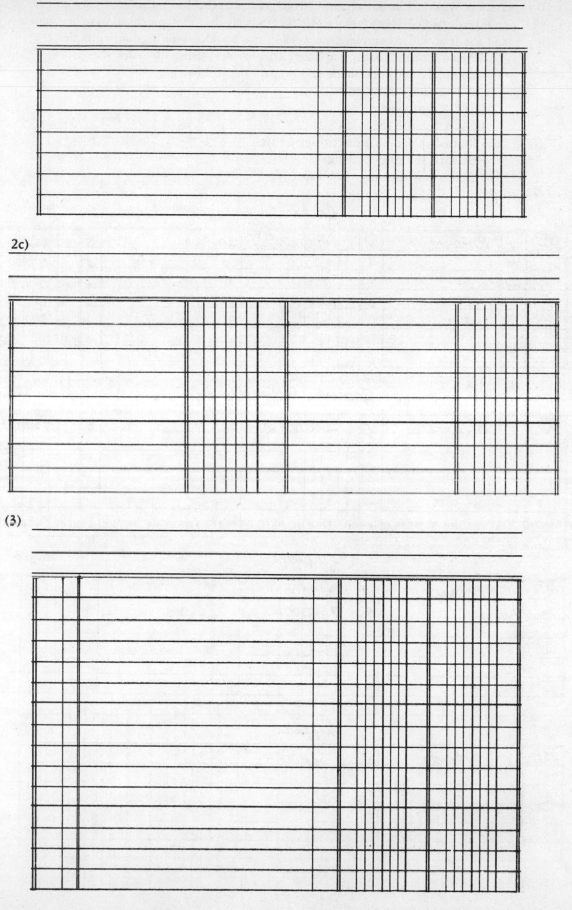

10–4 Pamela Washington is a recent college graduate who has started her own private accounting practice. Her journal and ledger indicate that all transactions have been posted, and she is about to complete the work of the bookkeeping/accounting cycle.

(1) Pencil-foot the ledger and take a trial balance, using the work sheet form.
(2) Complete the work sheet, and prepare the following:
    a) An income statement.
    b) A capital statement.
    c) A balance sheet.
(3) Journalize and post the closing entries.
(4) Balance and rule the ledger.
(5) Take a post-closing trial balance.

Cash   No. 11

198– Dec.	1	Balance	✓	1000 00	198– Dec.	20		5	250 00
	10		4	500 00		30		5	175 00
	22		5	750 00		31		6	100 00
			6	1350 00		31		6	90 00
						31		6	800 00

Accounts Receivable   No. 12

198– Dec.	1	Balance	✓	2000 00	198– Dec.	22		5	750 00

Equipment   No. 13

198– Dec.	1	Balance	✓	3500 00					
	15		4	1500 00					

Supplies   No. 14

198– Dec.	1	Balance	✓	580 00					

Accounts Payable No. 21

Date			PR	Amount	Date			PR	Amount
198– Dec.	20		5	250 00	198– Dec.	1	Balance	✓	450 00
						15		4	1500 00

Pamela Washington, Capital No. 31

Date			PR	Amount	Date			PR	Amount
					198– Dec.	1	Balance	✓	6630 00

Pamela Washington, Drawing No. 32

Date			PR	Amount	Date			PR	Amount
198– Dec.	31		6	800 00					

Revenue and Expense Summary No. 33

Date			PR	Amount	Date			PR	Amount

Fees Income No. 41

Date			PR	Amount	Date			PR	Amount
					198– Dec.	10		4	500 00
						31		6	1350 00

Automobile Expense   No. 51

198– Dec.	31		6	90 00					

Office Expense   No. 52

198– Dec.	31		6	100 00					

Rent Expense   No. 53

198– Dec.	30		5	175 00					

Account Title	A. N.	Trial Balance		Income Statement		Balance Sheet	
		Debit	Credit	Debit	Credit	Debit	Credit

Pamela Washington
Income Statement
For the Month Ended December 31, 198—

Pamela Washington
Capital Statement
For the Month Ended December 31, 198—

Pamela Washington
Balance Sheet
December 31, 198—

GENERAL JOURNAL   Page **7**

Date	Account Title	PR	Debit	Credit

Pamela Washington
Post-closing Trial Balance
December 31, 198-

THINK IT OVER

Len Green says he does not make closing entries, nor does he ever prepare a post-closing trial balance. He claims these steps are not needed because he uses only ten to twelve accounts. What difficulties will he encounter two or three fiscal periods from now, if he wishes to prepare financial statements? Do you think the Internal Revenue Service would approve of a tax return based on statements that confuse information from one fiscal period to the next?

CHAPTER **11**

CASH SYSTEMS, CHECKING ACCOUNTS

Most businesses make payments by checks drawn on local commercial banks. Many individuals now use checking accounts drawing on funds in savings banks and/or in money funds. A check is a written order directing the DRAWEE (the bank) to make payment to the PAYEE (the party indicated by the words "Pay to the order of") from the account balance of the DRAWER (the party who signs the order or check).

Opening a Checking Account

When a checking account is opened, each person authorized to sign checks completes a signature card. A deposit slip is used to list items to be added to the account, including checks received from others—paychecks, amounts collected from customers, and so on.

Endorsing Checks

Each check deposited must be endorsed, that is, signed on the back by the payee. There are several types of endorsements.

    (1)   An ENDORSEMENT IN BLANK. This is a simple signature of the depositor.

(2) A SPECIAL (or FULL) ENDORSEMENT. This states to whom a check is to be paid.

> *Pay to the order of*
> *Wilma Higgins*
> *Gordon J. Barnes*

(3) A RESTRICTIVE ENDORSEMENT. This limits the further purpose or use of the check.

> *For deposit only*
> *Acct. no. 831456*
> *Gordon J. Barnes*

(4) A QUALIFIED ENDORSEMENT. The endorser assumes no legal responsibility for payment, should the drawer have insufficient funds to honor his/her own check.

> *Without recourse*
> *Gordon J. Barnes*

The restrictive endorsement should be used on checks to be deposited. The blank endorsement should be used only when presenting a check for immediate payment, for example, when cashing one's paycheck.

Making Deposits

Assume that Gordon Barnes opens a checking account and completes the following deposit slip:

FOR DEPOSIT TO THE ACCOUNT OF		DOLLARS	CENTS
NAME *Gordon J. Barnes*	BILLS	250	00
ADDRESS *125 Main St. Bolton*	COINS	—	
DATE *Jan. 2* 198—	CHECKS AS FOLLOWS, PROPERLY ENDORSED	150	00
		500	00
BOLTON NATIONAL BANK New York, NY		375	00
CHECKS AND OTHER ITEMS ARE RECEIVED FOR DEPOSIT SUBJECT TO THE TERMS AND CONDITIONS OF THIS BANK'S COLLECTION AGREEMENT	TOTAL DEPOSIT	1,275	00

⑆0860⑈0830⑆1243⑈676⑈

His account balance will be $1,275, and that amount will be entered on his check stub record on the balance brought forward (Bal. Bro't For'd) line. As future deposits are made, he will add to find the total; as checks are drawn, he will subtract to find the balance carried forward (Bal. Car'd For'd).

Drawing Checks

Follow these stubs and checks completed by Barnes for each of these cash payment transactions:

January 2, 198–, Paid Ace Realty $250 for month's rent; check No. 101
5, 198–, Paid Security National Bank $300 on loan balance; check No. 102

(Be sure stubs are completed first, showing all information; then complete each check, using pen and ink.)

Stub No. 101

NO. *101* $*250.00*
DATE *Jan. 2* 19*8–*
TO *Ace Realty*
FOR *January rent*

	DOLLARS	CENTS
BAL. BRO'T FOR'D	1275	00
AMT. DEPOSITED		
TOTAL	1275	00
AMT. THIS CHECK	250	00
BAL. CAR'D FOR'D	1025	00

Check No. 101

No *101*
1-830 / 860

January 2 19*8–*

Pay to the order of *Ace Realty* $ *250.00*

Two hundred fifty & 00/100 Dollars

BOLTON NATIONAL BANK
of New York, NY

Gordon J. Barnes

⑈0860⑈0830⑈ 1243⑈671⑈

Stub No. 102

NO *102* $*300.00*
DATE *Jan. 5* 19*8–*
TO *Security National Bank*
FOR *loan payment*

	DOLLARS	CENTS
BAL. BRO'T FOR'D	1025	00
AMT. DEPOSITED		
TOTAL	1025	00
AMT. THIS CHECK	300	00
BAL. CAR'D FOR'D	725	00

Check No. 102

No *102*
1-830 / 860

January 5 19*8–*

Pay to the order of *Security National Bank* $ *300.00*

Three hundred & 00/100 Dollars

BOLTON NATIONAL BANK
of New York, NY

Gordon J. Barnes

⑈0860⑈0830⑈ 1243⑈671⑈

Notice that the balance carried forward from stub No. 101 is brought forward to stub No. 102. In this way, Barnes will always have a running balance in his checking account.

Each check stub will serve as the source of information for making a journal entry. The two entries for stubs No. 101 and No. 102 are illustrated as follows.

198–					
Jan.	2	Rent Expense		250 00	
		Cash			250 00
		Check No. 101			
	5	Security National Bank		300 00	
		Cash			300 00
		Check No. 102			

The Bank Statement

At the end of the month, or at a set date during each month, the bank sends each depositor a BANK STATEMENT. This is the bank's record of the deposits made, and the checks drawn *and presented for payment*. These checks are CANCELED—marked paid—and returned to the depositor with the bank statement. If any charges have been made by the bank for handling this account, they are identified as "SC" ("service charge") and deducted from the balance. The depositor makes a similar deduction on the next check stub.

Here is the entry Barnes makes in his journal for the service charge made on his statement at the end of the month:

31	Miscellaneous Expense			3 75			
	Cash					3 75	
	Bank Service Charge, Jan.						

Reconciling Check Stub Balance and Bank Statement

Frequently, the depositor's check stub balance and the checking account bank statement balance do not agree by the end of each month. There are several reasons for these differences.

(1) A late deposit, or a DEPOSIT IN TRANSIT, is added into the *check stub balance* but does not reach the bank in time to be recorded on the bank statement—*add any late or omitted deposits to the bank balance.*

(2) Some checks drawn and sent to distant points have not cleared back to the depositor's bank in time to be recorded on the bank statement—*subtract the amount of OUTSTANDING CHECKS from the bank balance.*

(3) If the bank made any service charges, they are deducted on the bank statement—*subtract the service charge on the check stub record.*

At this point, Barnes prepares a BANK RECONCILIATION STATEMENT to determine his correct, available checkbook and bank balance. This amount must be the same for both balances at any given time.

Gordon J. Barnes
Bank Reconciliation Statement
January 31, 198–

Checkbook Balance	675.00	Bank Balance	895.00
Deduct: Service		Add: Deposit in	
Charge	3.75	Transit	200.00
		Deduct: Outstanding	
		Checks	
		No. 119, 100.00	
		No. 120, 200.00	
		No. 121, 123.75	
			423.75
Correct Check Stub		Available Bank	
Balance	671.25	Balance	671.25

The amount of cash that Barnes has in his checking account, against which he can draw future checks, is $671.25. If he had not prepared this reconciliation, he might have OVERDRAWN his account. One or more of his checks might have been dishonored because of insufficient funds.

YOU SHOULD REMEMBER

Outstanding checks *reduce* a bank statement balance.
A bank reconciliation is necessary to avoid *overdrawing* one's checking account.

KNOW YOUR VOCABULARY

Bank reconciliation

Bank statement

Canceled

Deposit in transit

Drawee; drawer

Endorsement in blank

Full endorsement
(special)

Outstanding checks

Overdrawn

Payee

Qualified endorsement

Restrictive endorsement

QUESTIONS

1. Why is a check referred to as a "three-party instrument"?
2. How is a signature card used by the bank teller?
3. What entry is recorded for a bank service charge?
4. Why is a reconciliation statement necessary?

PROBLEMS

11–1   Complete Marian Moore's deposit slip for the following items:

23 twenty-dollar bills	18 quarters
48 ten-dollar bills	31 dimes
16 five-dollar bills	14 nickels
29 one-dollar bills	42 pennies
Checks: $148.65 and $79.15	

FOR DEPOSIT TO THE ACCOUNT OF		DOLLARS	CENTS
BILLS			
NAME _____ **COINS**			
ADDRESS _____ CHECKS AS FOLLOWS, PROPERLY ENDORSED			
DATE_____ 19___			
BOLTON NATIONAL BANK			
New York, NY			
CHECKS AND OTHER ITEMS ARE RECEIVED FOR DEPOSIT SUBJECT TO THE TERMS AND CONDITIONS OF THIS BANK'S COLLECTION AGREEMENT	**TOTAL DEPOSIT**		

⑈0860⑈0830⑈1843⑈671⑈

11–2   Louann Pringle, owner of a home cleaning service, completed the following checkbook transactions:

January 15,   Paid for cleaning supplies, $40; check No. 118
       19,   Paid for taxi service, $15; check No. 119
       22,   Deposited $75 in bills
       22,   Withdrew $50 for personal use; check No. 120

(1) Complete each stub and check, signing each check as Pringle would.
(2) Complete the deposit slip and enter the amount on the deposit line of the last check stub.

(1)

		DOLLARS	CENTS
NO._____ $_____			
DATE_____ 19___			
TO_____			
FOR_____			
_____			
BAL. BRO'T FOR'D		136	50
AMT. DEPOSITED			
TOTAL			
AMT. THIS CHECK			
BAL. CAR'D FOR'D			

No._____

1-830
___
860

_____ 19___

Pay to the
order of _____ $_____

_____ Dollars

BOLTON NATIONAL BANK
of New York, NY

⑊0860⑊0830⑊ 1848⑊671⑊

		DOLLARS	CENTS
NO._____ $_____			
DATE_____ 19___			
TO_____			
FOR_____			
_____			
BAL. BRO'T FOR'D			
AMT. DEPOSITED			
TOTAL			
AMT. THIS CHECK			
BAL. CAR'D FOR'D			

No._____

1-830
___
860

_____ 19___

Pay to the
order of _____ $_____

_____ Dollars

BOLTON NATIONAL BANK
of New York, NY

⑊0860⑊0830⑊ 1848⑊671⑊

(2)

FOR DEPOSIT TO THE ACCOUNT OF

NAME _____

ADDRESS _____

DATE_____ 19___

BOLTON NATIONAL BANK
New York, NY

CHECKS AND OTHER ITEMS ARE RECEIVED FOR DEPOSIT SUBJECT TO
THE TERMS AND CONDITIONS OF THIS BANK'S COLLECTION AGREEMENT.

	DOLLARS	CENTS
BILLS		
COINS		
CHECKS AS FOLLOWS, PROPERLY ENDORSED		
TOTAL DEPOSIT		

⑊0860⑊0830⑊1848⑊671⑊

(1)

	DOLLARS	CENTS
BAL. BRO'T FOR'D		
AMT. DEPOSITED		
TOTAL		
AMT. THIS CHECK		
BAL. CAR'D FOR'D		

NO._____ $_____
DATE_____ 19____
TO_____
FOR_____

No._____

1-830
860

19____

Pay to the
order of _____ $_____

_____ Dollars

BOLTON NATIONAL BANK
of New York, NY

⑊:0860⑈0830⑉: 1848⑈671⑈

11-3 Helen Spiro's last check stub balance was $420.90. Her bank statement balance dated November 30, 198— was $397.40. A $250 deposit was in transit on that date. Outstanding checks were as follows: No. 217, $75.00; No. 219, $105.50; No. 220, $50.00. The bank service charge for the month was $4.00. Prepare a reconciliation statement, indicating the correct checkbook balance and available bank balance on November 30.

Checkbook Balance	**Bank Balance**

11-4 Yoshi Kawahara, a landscape engineer, received his January bank statement on February 2. The balance was $626.66. His last check stub balance was $708.92. On comparing the two, he noted that a deposit of $375 made on January 31 was not included on the statement; also, a bank service charge of $3.60 was deducted. Outstanding checks were as follows: No. 641, $92.50; No. 644, $107.25; No. 646, $37.80; and No. 647, $58.79.

(1) Complete a reconciliation statement, indicating Kawahara's correct, available bank balance.
(2) Record the service charge in Kawahara's general journal.

(1)

Bank Reconciliation Statement	
Checkbook Balance	Bank Balance

(2)

THINK IT OVER

Timothy Hankins used a qualified endorsement in cashing a check that subsequently was dishonored because of insufficient funds. What rights does the bank cashing the check have? Who is liable for payment?

CHAPTER **12**

THE PETTY CASH FUND

Purpose of the Fund

All cash received by a business should be deposited promptly in a checking account. Also, withdrawals are usually made by issuing checks signed by an authorized officer of the business. In that way there is a record of all funds coming in (cash debit) and all funds paid out (cash credit). However, there are times when small amounts must be paid out, perhaps for postage stamps, a collect telegram, or a package delivered collect on delivery, for which drawing a check would not be practical.

A special PETTY CASH fund is maintained for these small payments. This fund requires strict control because of the danger of missing cash. The following procedures are recommended to safeguard the petty cash fund:

(1) Petty cash should be kept separately from any other cash on hand.
(2) One person only should be held responsible for the petty cash fund.
(3) A record of each payment from petty cash should be kept, showing the person to whom it was paid, the reason, the date, the amount, and, if possible, the signature of the person to whom it was given.

Establishing the Fund

To establish a petty cash fund, a check is drawn *payable to Petty Cash*, a new ledger account, directly following the Cash account.

NO. *376*　$ *40 00*
DATE *August 2* 198—
TO *Petty Cash*
FOR *to establish fund*

	DOLLARS	CENTS
BAL. BRO'T FOR'D	581	36
AMT. DEPOSITED	400	00
TOTAL	981	36
AMT. THIS CHECK	40	00
BAL. CAR'D FOR'D	941	36

ACE TRAVEL SERVICE

No. *376*

1-830
860

August 2 198—

Pay to the order of *Petty Cash*　　　$ *40 00*

Forty & 00/100 ~~~~~~~~~~~~~~~~~~~ Dollars

BOLTON NATIONAL BANK
of New York, NY

Hans Petersen

⑆0860⑈0830⑆ 1243⑈671⑈

The preceding check is endorsed by Hans Petersen and cashed. The amount is turned over to the person in charge of the fund, to be placed in a drawer or cash box, under lock and key. The check stub becomes the source document for the following journal entry:

198—						
aug.	2	Petty Cash			40 00	
		Cash				40 00
		To Establish Fund, Check No. 376				

Making Disbursements

Petty cash DISBURSEMENTS are made now whenever small amounts must be paid. The person requesting the amount may be required to fill out a numbered PETTY CASH VOUCHER, giving all required information and signing the voucher. The authorized signature is then obtained to make the disbursement from the fund. The voucher is filed or kept in a separate compartment of the fund box. The following is a typical petty cash voucher:

No. _____

ACE TRAVEL SERVICE
Petty Cash Voucher

Date _____ 19____

Pay to _____

For _____

Amount
$

Payment Received　　　Authorized

As the amount of petty cash remaining in the fund decreases, the dollar amount of the vouchers increases. At any time, the two taken together will total the *original amount in the fund*. When the petty cash fund balance gets low, it will be REPLENISHED by drawing another check payable to petty cash. The amount of this check will be exactly *equal to the total of the vouchers*. The check is cashed, and the money is placed in the petty cash drawer or box. Once again, the petty cash fund equals the total amount for which the fund was established originally.

Assume that petty cash vouchers indicate that payments were made over a period of time for many items. These vouchers are sorted out as follows:

Office expenses	$17.50	
Delivery expenses	9.60	
Miscellaneous expenses	5.95	$33.05

Proving Petty Cash

To *prove petty cash* at this point, the remaining cash is counted. Since the fund started with $40, there should be $6.95 remaining in the petty cash fund. This proves correct:

$40.00	(original balance)
− 33.05	(disbursements)
$ 6.95	(cash fund count)

The replenishing check stub and check are shown below:

			ACE TRAVEL SERVICE	No. 387
NO. 387	$ 33 05			1-830 / 860
DATE August 31 198—				
TO Petty Cash			August 31 198—	
FOR Replenish fund:			Pay to the order of Petty Cash	$33 05
Off. Supp. $17.50; Del. Exp. $9.60; Misc. Exp. $5.95			Thirty-three + 05/100 ———— Dollars	
	DOLLARS	CENTS		
BAL. BRO'T FOR'D	642	79		
AMT. DEPOSITED			BOLTON NATIONAL BANK	
			of New York, NY	Hans Petersen
TOTAL	642	79		
AMT. THIS CHECK	33	05		
BAL. CAR'D FOR'D	609	74	⑈0860⑈0830⑉ 1243⑈671⑈	

Replenishing the Fund

The replenishing entry prepared from the check stub will result in a debit to the various items for which petty cash has been disbursed. In that way *the only debit to the petty cash account is from the entry to establish the fund*; that will remain the account balance, unless the fund is changed. The items for which petty cash was spent will be posted to the specific accounts for which petty cash was disbursed.

	31	Delivery Expense						9	60				
		Miscellaneous Expense						5	95				
		Office Expense					1	7	50				
		Cash									33	05	
		To Replenish Petty Cash,											
		Check No. 387											

Petty cash should be replenished at least once each month, usually at the end of the month, or the end of a fiscal period, and whenever the fund runs low.

YOU SHOULD REMEMBER

Only *one person* should be *responsible for a petty cash fund.*

The *sum of all vouchers* (for which disbursements have been made) *plus cash* in the petty cash fund must *equal the original amount* of the fund.

The *replenishing entry* debits the *accounts* for which petty cash was disbursed.

Only *one amount* appears as a *debit in the petty cash account—the amount* for which it was *established.*

KNOW YOUR VOCABULARY

Disbursements	Petty cash voucher
Petty cash	Replenish

QUESTIONS

1. Why is it recommended procedure to have one person in charge of the petty cash fund?
2. What is the source document for the *entry* to establish petty cash? To replenish petty cash?
3. What is the journal entry to establish petty cash?
4. What is the journal entry to replenish petty cash?
5. How is petty cash proved?

PROBLEMS

12–1 Hilda Marcello, owner of Space Travel Services, has decided to establish a petty cash fund because of frequent, small disbursements.

   (1) Draw a check for $35 to establish the fund.

   (2) As the authorized person, complete petty cash vouchers for each of the following disbursements:

   April 2, $2.75 to messenger who delivered a package (delivery expense)
        9, $8.00 for postage (office expense)
      16, $10.00 gasoline for auto (auto expense)
      23, $7.50 for printing business cards (miscellaneous expense)
      30, $4.00 for postage

   (3) Sort these vouchers; prove petty cash; complete a check stub and check to replenish the petty cash fund on the last day of the month.

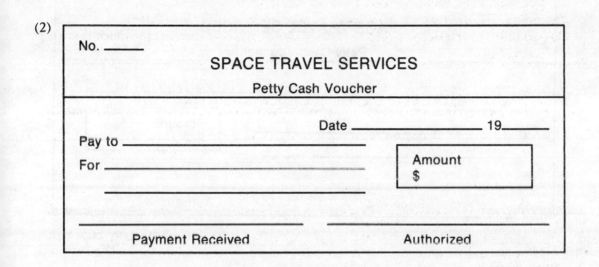

	DOLLARS	CENTS
O. *138* $		
ATE 19		
O		
OR		
AL. BRO'T FOR'D	*1406*	*92*
AMT. DEPOSITED		
TOTAL		
MT. THIS CHECK		
AL. CAR'D FOR'D		

SPACE TRAVEL SERVICES

No.

1-830
—————
860

_____ 19____

Pay to the
order of _____ $ _____

_____ Dollars

BOLTON NATIONAL BANK
of New York, NY

⑈0860⑈0830⑈ 1243⑈671⑈

(2)

No. _____

SPACE TRAVEL SERVICES

Petty Cash Voucher

Date _____ 19_____

Pay to _____

For _____   Amount
                                  $

_____

Payment Received   Authorized

No. _____

SPACE TRAVEL SERVICES

Petty Cash Voucher

Date _____ 19_____

Pay to _____

For _____   Amount
                                  $

_____

Payment Received   Authorized

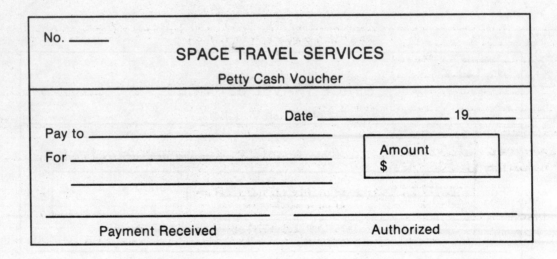

REPLENISHING THE FUND   107

No. _____

SPACE TRAVEL SERVICES

Petty Cash Voucher

Date _____ 19_____

Pay to _____

For _____

Amount
$

_____

Payment Received   **Authorized**

---

3)

NO. _156_____ $_____

DATE_____ 19_____

TO_____

FOR_____

_____

	DOLLARS	CENTS
BAL. BRO'T FOR'D	1091	97
AMT. DEPOSITED	500	00
TOTAL	1591	37
AMT. THIS CHECK		
BAL. CAR'D FOR'D		

SPACE TRAVEL SERVICES

No._____

1-315
860

_____ 19_____

Pay to the
order of _____ $_____

_____ Dollars

BOLTON NATIONAL BANK
of Long Island, NY

⑆0860⑈0830⑆ 1243⑈671⑈

12-2 Using the information in Problem 12-1 (1) and (3), complete the journal entries to establish the petty cash fund and to replenish it.

GENERAL JOURNAL   Page 15

Date	Account Title	PR	Debit	Credit

THINK IT OVER

Connie's Interior Designs has a $50 petty cash fund. The owner's assistant, Jim Landers, is authorized to draw checks from the regular checking account and is also in charge of the petty cash fund. Last month, disbursements from the fund increased, and the fund had to be replenished several times. What recommendations might be made to the owner regarding the control factor, as well as the amount in the fund?

CYCLE ONE
EXAMINATION

Part I Indicate by a check (√) in the column at the right whether each statement is TRUE or FALSE.

	T	F
Example: All accounts increase by debits.		√
1. Liabilities and owner's equity increase by credits.	√	
2. For every transaction, increases equal decreases.		√
3. For every transaction, debits equal credits.	√	
4. A debit to the Cash account results in an increase.	√	
5. A debit to J. Smith, Capital, results in an increase.		√
6. A journal entry is posted to ledger accounts.	√	
7. The ledger account PR column indicates the journal page number.	√	
8. A balance sheet describes the financial operations over a period of time.		√
9. An income statement is a picture of the financial condition of a business.		√
10. The omission of a transaction will cause a trial balance to be out of balance.		√
11. A $100 debit posted as a credit will cause Trial Balance columns to differ by $200.	√	
12. A work sheet aids in the preparation of financial statements.	√	
13. A capital statement starts with owner's equity at the end of the fiscal period.		√
14. Closing entries result in zero balances in revenue and expense accounts.	√	
15. A net loss for the fiscal period is closed into the capital account by a debit to Revenue and Expense Summary and a credit to the capital account.		√
16. Balance sheet accounts normally have balances that carry over to succeeding fiscal periods.	√	
17. A check stub should be completed before writing the check.	√	
18. A bank statement balance will identify the checks that are outstanding.		√
19. Each petty cash voucher is the source document for a journal entry.	√	√
20. The petty cash fund replenishing entry results in debits to the various accounts for which petty cash was spent.	√	

Part II Match the definition with the term by writing the appropriate *letter* in the column at the right. (A term is used once only.)

Terms		Definitions		Letter
		Example: The value in an account		C
A.	Accounts receivable	1. A simple signature on the back of a check	1.	I
B.	Asset	2. All accounts arranged by number	2.	L
C.	Balance	3. Transferring entries from the journal to accounts	3.	Q
D.	Bank statement	4. A listing of all accounts with debit or credit balances for a work sheet	4.	U
E.	Closing entry			
F.	Creditor	5. The one to whom a debt is owed	5.	F
G.	Disbursement	6. Payments made from the petty cash fund	6.	G
H.	Drawee			
I.	Endorsement in blank	7. A statement prepared to find the correct checkbook and bank balance	7.	R
J.	Income statement	8. Income earned	8.	T
K.	Journal	9. Any form used as a source document for a transaction	9.	V
L.	Ledger			
M.	Liabilities	10. A journal entry that zeros out an account balance	10.	E
N.	Owner's equity	11. Anything of value owned	11.	B
O.	Payee	12. Net worth or capital	12.	N
P.	Post-closing trial balance	13. Customers' accounts	13.	A
Q.	Posting	14. A chronological list of transactions, as a diary	14.	K
R.	Reconciliation statement			
S.	Restrictive endorsement	15. The bank on which a check is drawn	15.	H
T.	Revenue			
U.	Trial balance			
V.	Voucher			

Part III   For each of the following transactions, indicate the accounts to be debited and credited. Use the account titles listed at the left.

Account Titles	Transactions		Account Dr.	Account Cr.
A. Cash	*Example:* Received $100 fee from customer.		A	G
B. Supplies	1. Paid employee salary, $200.	1.	J	A
C. Accounts Payable	2. Bought $30 worth of supplies for cash.	2.	B	A
D. J. Owner, Capital	3. Invested $1,000 cash.	3.	A	D
E. J. Owner, Drawing	4. Closed the revenue account.	4.	G	F
F. Revenue and Expense Summary	5. Bought $500 worth of supplies, paying $100 down, and balance on account.	5.	B	A/C
G. Commissions Income	6. Withdrew $150 cash for personal use.	6.	E	A
H. Auto Expense	7. Closed the expense accounts	7.	F	H/I/J
I. Miscellaneous Expense	8. Closed net income to owner's equity.	8.	F	D
J. Salary Expense	9. Closed net loss to owner's equity.	9.	D	F
	10. Closed the drawing account	10.	D	E

Part IV (1) Complete Chet Gorski's work sheet.
       (2) Complete a capital statement; assume that Gorski made a $5,000 investment during the year.
       (3) Complete a balance sheet.
       (4) Journalize the closing entries.

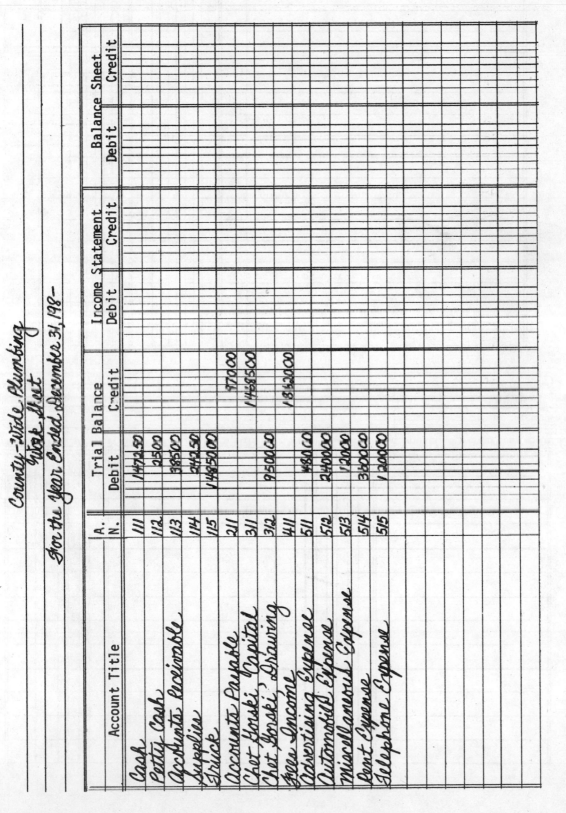

County-Wide Plumbing
Work Sheet
For the Year Ended December 31, 198—

Account Title	A.N.	Trial Balance Debit	Trial Balance Credit	Income Statement Debit	Income Statement Credit	Balance Sheet Debit	Balance Sheet Credit
Cash	111	1472.50					
Petty Cash	112	2500					
Accounts Receivable	113	38502					
Supplies	114	242.50					
Truck	115	1485000					
Accounts Payable	211		77000				
Chet Gorski, Capital	311		1458500				
Chet Gorski's Drawing	312	950000					
Gross Income	411		1813000				
Advertising Expense	511	48060					
Automobile Expense	512	240000					
Miscellaneous Expense	513	12000					
Rent Expense	514	360000					
Telephone Expense	515	130000					

(2) _____

(3) _____

GENERAL JOURNAL Page **7**

Part V (1) Complete the following check stub and check:

	DOLLARS	CENTS
NO. *207* $ *35.50*		
DATE *January 7* 19*8—*		
TO *Wilson Supply Co.*		
FOR *Smoke alarm*		
(Equipment)		
	DOLLARS	CENTS
BAL. BRO'T FOR'D	382	47
AMT. DEPOSITED	225	00
TOTAL		
AMT. THIS CHECK		
BAL. CAR'D FOR'D		

No. _____

1-315 / 860

_____ 19 _____

Pay to the
order of _____ $ _____

_____ Dollars

BOLTON NATIONAL BANK
of Long Island, NY

⑈0860⑈0830⑈ 1248⑈671⑈

(2) Record the journal entry for the above payment to Wilson Supply Company for the purchase of equipment.

CYCLE TWO
A Merchandising Business

CHAPTER **13**

PURCHASES OF MERCHANDISE

Purchasing on Account—Accounts Payable

A merchandising business buys goods for resale to its customers; these goods are its MERCHANDISE. The usual procedure for most businesses is to buy ON ACCOUNT, rather than for cash. The balance is paid sometime in the future, perhaps within 30 to 60 days. As a result of such purchases, debts, called ACCOUNTS PAYABLE, are owed to creditors.

Purchases Journal

When many such purchases on account occur, it is preferred practice to record these transactions in a separate, special journal—a PURCHASES JOURNAL. This journal is used exclusively for recording one type of transaction—a *purchase of merchandise on account*.

   This expense or *cost of merchandise* creates a new account, Purchases. Like expenses, *cost accounts increase by debits and decrease by credits*. If this entry appeared in *general journal* form, it would look as follows:

198-					
Feb.	2	Purchases		500 00	
		Accounts Payable /B. Winslow ✓			500 00
		Purchases Invoice No. 152			

If there were many purchases of merchandise on account during a fiscal period, this entry would be repeated, and each entry would be posted to the Purchases account as well as the Accounts Payable account. (Purchases would be numbered 51; Accounts Payable would be numbered 21; all expenses would be renumbered, starting with 61.)

Posting Creditors' Accounts

To eliminate this repetitive posting to both Purchases and Accounts Payable, a PURCHASES JOURNAL is used. Creditors' accounts are posted for all entries so that up-to-date balances will be available. These accounts are located in a separate accounts payable ledger—a SUBSIDIARY LEDGER—where they are arranged alphabetically, or in some cases by special account number. Examine the following purchases journal entries:

PURCHASES JOURNAL   Page 6

Date		From Whom Purchased - Account Credited	Invoice No.	PR	Purchases Dr. Accts. Pay. Cr.
198– apr.	2	Tri-Royal Sales Company	4834		3096 00
	7	Thomas Gregorius + Sons	045		375 00
	19	Vincent Morock, Inc.	380		400 00
	26	Thomas Gregorius + Sons	061		250 00

Each of these entries originated with a source document, an INVOICE, a statement or bill completed by the seller of merchandise. As can be seen from the following invoice, this form contains a complete description of the transaction. When received, it is checked against the merchandise that was shipped. Then it is recorded in the special purchases journal. Tri-Royal *sold* merchandise to Best-West and prepared the following invoice. Best-West *bought* merchandise from Tri-Royal and received a copy of that invoice, from which the purchases journal entry is made.

TRI-ROYAL SALES COMPANY
2158 Chambers Street
Trenton, NJ 08609

Sold to
Best-West Sewing Machine Corp   Invoice No. 4834
296 South Street   Date *April 2, 198–*
Newark, NJ 07114   Our Order No. 7985
                                     Customer's Order No. 924
Terms 30 *days*   Shipped via *Truck*

Quantity	Description	Unit Price	Total Amount
18	EZ Sewing Machines #A15	145 75	2623 50
75	Hooks #H107	6 30	472 50
			3096 00

Summarizing the Purchases Journal

The purchases journal is posted on a regular basis to creditors' accounts in the subsidiary ledger. At the end of the month, this journal is SUMMARIZED—totaled and ruled, and the total is posted to the accounts named in the column headed "Purchases Dr. and Accounts Payable Cr." These accounts are in the GENERAL LEDGER. In this way, the general ledger maintains debits equal to credits.

Review the purchases journal below, which has now been posted to both subsidiary and general ledger accounts:

PURCHASES JOURNAL   Page 6

Date	From Whom Purchased - Account Credited	Invoice No.	PR	Purchases Dr. Accts. Pay. Cr.
198— apr. 2	Tri-Royal Sales Company	4834	✓	3096 00
7	Thomas Gregorius + Sons	045	✓	375 00
19	Vincent Nurock, Inc.	380	✓	400 00
26	Thomas Gregorius + Sons	061	✓	250 00
30	Total			4121 00
				(51) (21)

ACCOUNTS PAYABLE LEDGER

Thomas Gregorius + Sons
515 Capital Avenue, Trenton, N.J. 07114

Date		PR	Dr.	Cr.	Cr. Bal.
198— apr. 7		P6		375 00	375 00
26		P6		250 00	625 00

Vincent Nurock, Inc.
170 Underhill Boulevard, Syosset, NY 11791

Date		PR	Dr.	Cr.	Cr. Bal.
'98— mar. 4		P5		150 00	150 00
apr. 19		P6		400 00	550 00

Tri-Royal Sales Company
2158 Chambers Street, Trenton, NJ 08609

Date		PR	Dr.	Cr.	Cr. Bal.
'98— Feb. 28		P4		100 00	100 00
mar. 18		P5		200 00	300 00
apr. 2		P6		3096 00	3396 00

GENERAL LEDGER

Accounts Payable   No. 21

Date			PR	Dr.	Cr.	Balance Dr.	Balance Cr.
198– Feb. 28			P4		100 00		100 00
Mar. 31			P5		350 00		450 00
Apr. 30			P6		4121 00		4571 00

Purchases   No. 51

				Dr.	Cr.	Balance Dr.	Balance Cr.
198– Apr. 30			P6	4121 00		4121 00	

The creditors' postings are indicated by check marks (√) in the purchases journal because these accounts have no numbers—they are arranged alphabetically. The journal total was posted to accounts No. 51 and No. 21 (Purchases and Accounts Payable).

In the accounts payable ledger, note carefully the three-column arrangement of creditors' accounts, some of which have balances carried over from prior months. A credit posting increases an account with a credit balance. We will see in Chapter 14 that posting debits to these accounts decreases their balances.

As stated above, posting references to creditors' accounts are indicated by check marks in the purchases journal because they have no account numbers. The journal total is posted to general ledger accounts and is indicated as accounts No. 51 and No. 21. This same technique for posting will be used whenever special journals are involved.

Schedule of Accounts Payable

At the end of the month, the accuracy of postings can be proved by preparing a SCHEDULE OF ACCOUNTS PAYABLE. This is a listing of creditors' accounts and the balance owed to each creditor. The total of the schedule should be equal to the balance in the CONTROLLING ACCOUNT—Accounts Payable—which shows in *total* balance the sum of the individual subsidiary account balances.

Best-West Sewing Machine Company
Schedule of Accounts Payable
April 30, 198–

Thomas Gregorius & Sons	625 00
Vincent Nurock, Inc.	550 00
Tri-Royal Sales Company	3396 00
Total Accounts Payable	4571 00

YOU SHOULD REMEMBER

A purchases journal is a *book of original* entry, used only to record transactions for the *purchases of merchandise on account*.

The purchases journal *summary entry* posting is a *debit* to *Purchases* and a *credit* to *Accounts Payable*.

The schedule of accounts payable *total* equals the *balance* of the *Accounts Payable account*.

KNOW YOUR VOCABULARY

Accounts Payable	Purchases journal
Controlling account	Schedule of accounts payable
General ledger	Subsidiary ledger
Merchandise	Summarize (summary entry)
On account	

QUESTIONS

1. How does one distinguish between a service-type business and a merchandising business?
2. What type of transaction is recorded in a purchases journal?
3. How are creditors' accounts arranged in a subsidiary ledger?
4. How is the equality of general ledger debits and credits maintained when a special journal is used?
5. Why are creditors' accounts arranged alphabetically in a subsidiary ledger rather than numbered?
6. How is the accuracy of the subsidiary ledger proved?
7. What advantage is there in using a three-column ruling in creditors' accounts? A four-column ruling in general ledger accounts?

PROBLEMS

13–1 (1) Record the following purchases of merchandise on account on purchases journal page 5:

    February 3, 198– Dye & Akins, invoice No. 1705, $300
          10,   Edward Kalpakian & Sons, invoice No. G-116, $425
          17,   Dye & Akins, invoice No. 1751, $385
          25,   Edward Kalpakian & Sons, invoice No. G-151, $500

(2) Post to the subsidiary ledger.

(3) Summarize the purchases journal at the end of the month, and post to the general ledger.

(4) Prepare a schedule of accounts payable for the owner, Ruth Ann Davis.

(1)   PURCHASES JOURNAL   Page 2

(2)   *Dye and Akins*

| 198–Jan. 15 | | P1 | | 450 00 | 450 0 |

Kalpakian & Sons

GENERAL JOURNAL
Accounts Payable   No. 21

(3)

			Dr.	Cr.	Balance Dr.	Cr.
198–Jan. 31		P1		450 00		450 0

Purchases   No. 5

			Dr.	Cr.	Balance Dr.	Cr.

(4) _____

13-2 (1) Record the following purchases of merchandise on account:

February 1, 198–	Paul Olins, invoice No. 42, $175
5,	Wilson & Shea, invoice No. 513, $200
8,	Island Supply, invoice No. 72A, $265
12,	Wilson & Shea, invoice No. 543, $400
15,	Glen Mfg., Inc., invoice No. 31, $620
19,	Paul Olins, invoice No. 78, $360
22,	Gregory Sims, invoice No. 318, $250
26,	Island Supply, invoice No. 29B, $300

(2) Post to the subsidiary ledger.

(3) Summarize the purchases journal at the end of the month, and post to the general ledger.

(4) Prepare a schedule of accounts payable for the owner, Paul Zagretti.

1)

PURCHASES JOURNAL Page 2

ACCOUNTS PAYABLE LEDGER

Glen Mfg., Inc.

(2)

Island Supply

Paul Olins

Gregory Sims

Wilson & Shea

GENERAL LEDGER

Accounts Payable   No. 21

			Dr.	Cr.	Balance	
					Dr.	Dr.

Purchases   No. 51

			Dr.	Cr.	Balance	
					Dr.	Cr.

(4)

THINK IT OVER

By using a purchases journal, Harold Marino estimates that he saves at least one hour of posting time each week. How is this possible?

CHAPTER **14**

CASH DISBURSEMENTS JOURNAL

A great number of business transactions involve the payment of cash, mostly by check. Such cash disbursements occur when invoices for merchandise purchased on account are paid, as well as payments for equipment, supplies, rent, salaries, and so on.

With each cash disbursement, a credit to cash must be recorded to decrease the Cash account. For each of these transactions, there also is a debit to the other account(s) involved. A typical *general journal* entry for a cash disbursement follows:

198-				
Mar. 2	Accounts Payable / John Reid Co /	54000	
	Cash		54000
	Invoice No. 579, Check No. 318		

Columnar Journal —Special Columns

A general journal entry such as this requires postings to all accounts—Accounts Payable Debit, Cash Credit (in the general ledger), and John Reid Company's account debit (in the subsidiary ledger). It is preferable, therefore, to use a special CASH DISBURSEMENTS JOURNAL,

129

which will require less frequent and fewer postings, and still keep creditors' accounts up to date. The entry shown above has been recorded in Peter Frazzini's special journal, along with other typical cash disbursements transactions:

CASH DISBURSEMENTS JOURNAL   Page 1

Date	Account Debited	Ck. No.	PR	General Dr.	Accts. Pay. Dr.	Cash Cr.
198- mar. 2	John Reid Company	318			540 00	540 00
3	Rent Expense	319		300 00		300 00
9	Supplies	320		75 00		75 00
15	Salary Expense	321		150 00		150 00
16	Union National Bank	322			400 00	400 00
30	Jose Garcia, Drawing	323		500 00		500 00
31	Los Angeles Distributing Co.	324			495 00	495 00

Note that there is a special column for the controlling account—Accounts Payable Dr. While postings are required for each account debited, *special column totals are posted only at the end of the month.* This journal is summarized, and the columns that have *identifiable account title headings* are posted as indicated—Accounts Payable Dr. (21) and Cash Cr. (11). The General Dr. column total is not posted and checked (√) because there is no *single* general ledger account for that total. Furthermore, the individual accounts listed as debited will have been posted.

Summarizing the Journal

Frazzini's journal now appears as shown below, summarized and posted:

CASH DISBURSEMENTS JOURNAL   Page 1

Date	Account Debited	Ck. No.	PR	General Dr.	Accts. Pay Dr.	Cash Cr.
198- mar. 2	John Reid Company	318	√		540 00	540 00
3	Rent Expense	319	54	300 00		300 00
9	Supplies	320	14	75 00		75 00
15	Salary Expense	321	55	150 00		150 00
16	Union National Bank	322	√		400 00	400 00
30	Jose Garcia, Drawing	323	32	500 00		500 00
31	Los Angeles Distributing Co.	324	√		495 00	495 00
31	Totals			1035 00	1435 00	2460 00
				(√)	(21)	(11)

First the columns were pencil footed; debit totals equal credit totals. Then they were written in ink, and the journal was double ruled. The General Dr. column total is always checkmarked, and the special column totals have been posted to the accounts identified in their headings. The postings to creditors' accounts and to the Cash and Accounts Payable accounts follow (General Dr. column account postings are not illustrated here):

GENERAL LEDGER

Cash   No. 11

198-				Dr.	Cr.	Balance Dr.	Balance Cr.
Mar.	31		CR	500000		500000	
	31		CD1		246000	254000	

Accounts Payable   No. 21

198-				Dr.	Cr.	Balance Dr.	Balance Cr.
Mar.	1	Balance	✓				54000
	31		P1		199500		253500
	31		CD1	143500			110000

ACCOUNTS PAYABLE LEDGER

Los Angeles Distributing Company
5001 Santa Monica Boulevard, Los Angeles, CA 90002

198-				Cr.	Balance Dr.	Balance Cr.
Mar.	4	P1			49500	49500
	25	P1			100000	149500
	31	CD1	49500			100000

John Reed Company
72-05 Canyon Boulevard, Pasadena, CA 91100

198-					Cr.	Balance Dr.	Balance Cr.
Mar.	1	Balance	✓				54000
	2		CD1	54000			—

Union National Bank
452 Ocean Boulevard, San Diego, CA 92101

198-				Cr.	Balance Dr.	Balance Cr.
Mar.	15	P1			50000	50000
	31	CD1	40000			10000

Schedule of Accounts Payable

At the end of the month, Peter Frazzini's schedule of accounts payable is taken to prove the accuracy of the subsidiary ledger:

Peter Frazzini
Schedule of Accounts Payable
March 31, 198–

Los Angeles Distributing Co.	1 000 00
Union National Bank	100 00
Total Accounts Payable	1 100 00

The balance of the controlling account, Accounts Payable, is also $1,100. The two are equal; the subsidiary ledger proves.

A cash disbursements journal may be expanded to include four or more columns, depending on the needs of the business. For example, if many *cash purchases* of merchandise occur, a special column—*Purchases Dr.*—can be included. Some businesses find it convenient to include a *Salary Expense Dr.* column as well. If these columns are included, it is necessary to checkmark (√) the posting reference column; no posting is needed for each cash purchases entry, inasmuch as *the column total will be posted*, along with all other special column totals, *at the end of the month*.

Examine these entries in a five-column cash disbursements journal:

CASH DISBURSEMENTS JOURNAL   Page 4

		Account Debited	Ck. No. PR	General Dr.	Accts. Pay. Dr.	Purchases Dr.	Salary Exp. Dr.	Cash Cr.
198– mar.	4	Rent Expense	506	400 00				400 00
	7	Salary Expense	507 √				250 00	250 00
	12	Purchases	508 √			725 00		725 00
	19	Supplies Company	509		75 00			75 00
	26	Purchases	510 √			300 00		300 00
	31	Totals		400 00	75 00	1 025 00	250 00	1 750 00
				(√)	( )	( )	( )	( )

At the end of the month, the bookkeeping/accounting clerk can easily see which items need to be posted, and which do not. Those that are already checked *will not be posted*; items appearing in the *General Dr.* and *Accounts Payable Dr.* columns *will be posted* to the accounts identified in the account column. The *special column totals*—Accounts Payable Dr., Purchases Dr., Salary Expense Dr., and Cash Cr.—will be posted.

Source Document for Cash Disbursement

The cash disbursements journal, a multicolumn book of original entry, is used exclusively for entries that result in cash credits, which will cause a decrease in the amount of cash. For each entry, a check stub is identified as the source document in the Check Number (Ck. No.) column.

YOU SHOULD REMEMBER

Creditors' account balances should be kept up to date by frequent postings (daily or weekly).

Special journal column *totals* are *posted* to the accounts identified *in the column heading.*

KNOW YOUR VOCABULARY

Cash disbursements journal   Summary entry

QUESTIONS

1. What advantage is there to using special journals for cash disbursements transactions, compared to using the general journal?
2. How are postings from a cash disbursements journal identified in the general ledger account?
3. What justifies the use of a special column in a cash disbursements journal?
4. How are postings to subsidiary ledger accounts indicated in the cash disbursements journal?
5. When does the check mark (√) indicate not to post?
6. When does the check mark indicate that the item has been posted?
7. How is the accuracy of the subsidiary ledger proved?

PROBLEMS

14-1   Sid Krasnoff uses a four column cash disbursements journal with a special column for his personal cash withdrawals. Last month, his check stub record indicated the following:

March 1,   Paid month's rent, $400; check No. 247
    3,   Paid utilities bill, $76.50; check No. 248
    8,   Paid Paula Cory on account, $50; check No. 249
    10,   Withdrew for personal use, $500; check No. 250
    17,   Paid employee's salary, $300; check No. 251
    22,   Paid Hilda Piper on account, $90; check No. 252
    24,   Withdrew for personal use, $500; check No. 253
    29,   Bought new equipment, $1,250; check No. 254
    31,   Paid employee's salary, $300; check No. 255

(1) Record each of these transactions, checking any entry that is not to be posted separately.

(2) Summarize the cash disbursements journal, checking any *total that is not to be posted*. Indicate by open parentheses ( ) totals that would be posted.

(1) and (2)   **CASH DISBURSEMENTS JOURNAL**   Page **3**

Date	Account Debited	Ck. No.	PR	General Dr.	Acct. Pay. Dr.	S. Krasnoff Draw. Dr.	Cash Cr.

14–2   Helen Scordas uses a special purchases journal and a three-column cash disbursements journal. Last month, she completed the following transactions:

April 1, Paid month's rent, $450; check No. 502
      4, Purchased merchandise on account from Abel & Jenks, $600; invoice No. P-311
      8, Withdrew for personal use $400; check No. 503
     14, Paid Abel & Jenks on account $800; check No. 504
     15, Paid employee's salary, $325; check No. 505
     20, Purchased merchandise on account from W. T. Gross, $1,450; invoice No. 5113
     22, Bought supplies, $75; check No. 506
     28, Withdrew for personal use, $500; check No. 507
     30, Paid W. T. Gross part on account, $725; check No. 508

(1) Record the entries for each transaction.
(2) Post the entries from the purchases journal.
(3) Post the entries from the cash disbursements journal.
(4) Summarize each journal, and post the column totals as indicated in the headings of each special column.
(5) Prove the accuracy of the subsidiary ledger by preparing a schedule of accounts payable.

(1) and (4)   PURCHASES JOURNAL   Page **2**

Date	Account Credited		Inv. No.	PR	Purchases Dr. Acct. Pay. Cr.

and (4)   CASH DISBURSEMENTS JOURNAL   Page 3

Date	Acct. Dr.	Ck. No.	PR	General Dr.	Acct. Pay. Dr.	Cash Cr.

Supplies   No. 13

Date		PR	Dr.	Cr.	Balance Dr.	Balance Cr.

GENERAL LEDGER

Accounts Payable   No. 21

and (3)

Date		PR	Dr.	Cr.	Balance Dr.	Balance Cr.
98- pr. 1	Balance	✓				80000

Helen Scordas, Drawing   No. 32

Date		PR	Dr.	Cr.	Balance Dr.	Balance Cr.

Purchases   No. 51

Date		PR	Dr.	Cr.	Balance Dr.	Balance Cr.

Rent Expense

No. 61

Date			PR	Dr.	Cr.	Balance Dr.	Cr.

Salary Expense

No. 62

Date			PR	Dr.	Cr.	Balance Dr.	Cr.

ACCOUNTS PAYABLE LEDGER

(2) and (3)   *Abel & Jenks*
1200 Mineral Boulevard, Scranton, PA 18501

				Dr.	Cr.	Cr. Bal.
198-Apr. 1	Balance		✓			800 00

W. F. Gross
805 Keystone Road, Wilkes Barre, PA 18700

				Dr.	Cr.	Cr. Bal.

(5)

THINK IT OVER

Laura Lan uses a purchases journal, a columnar cash payments journal, and a general journal to record the transactions occurring in her business. What types of entries does she record in each journal? She is considering using other special journals, as well. What might be her reasons?

WORDS TO REMEMBER
Sales Journal a special journal to record transactions only for *the sale of merchandise on account*
Schedule of Accounts Receivable an end-of-month list of *all customers* and the *amount due from each*

CHAPTER **15**

SALES OF MERCHANDISE

Sales on Account

For a merchandising business, the sale of merchandise is probably the most frequent of all transactions. In many large businesses, a major part of sales are ON ACCOUNT, that is, credit sales.

A general journal entry to record the sale of merchandise on account follows:

198-					
Apr.	7	Accounts Receivable/Alan Bergstrom	✓	175 00	
		Sales			175 00
		Sales Invoice No. 251			

Sales Journal and Accounts Receivable Ledger

If there were many sales similar to this one during a fiscal period, this entry would be repeated, and each entry would be posted to the Accounts Receivable account as well as to the Sales account. To eliminate the repetitive posting to both Accounts Receivable and Sales, a SALES

137

JOURNAL is used. Customers' accounts are posted for each entry so that up-to-date balances will be available. These accounts are located in another *separate subsidiary ledger*—an ACCOUNTS RECEIVABLE LEDGER—where accounts may be arranged alphabetically or, in some cases, by special account number. Examine the following sales journal entries:

SALES JOURNAL   Page

Date	To Whom Sold - Account Debited	Invoice No.	PR	Accts. Rec.Dr. Sales Cr.
198- apr. 2	Best-West Sewing Machine Company	4834		3096 00
9	Elaine K. Brown	4835		175 00
23	Ralph Mazel & Company	4836		250 00
30	Elaine K. Brown	4837		200 00

Source Documents for Sales Journal Entries

Each of these entries originated with a source document, the invoice or sales slip, completed by the salesperson or the billing department of the seller. This invoice is prepared in TRIPLICATE copy; one copy is given to the customer, one copy is used by the shipping department, and one copy is sent to the accounting department for a source document to record the transaction. (Refer to the invoice on page 120: Tri-Royal Sales Company is the seller; Best-West Sewing Machine Company is the buyer, or the customer.)

Posting and Summarizing the Sales Journal

The sales journal is posted on a regular basis to customers' accounts in the subsidiary ledger. At the end of the month, this journal, like all special journals, is summarized, and the total is posted to the accounts named in the columns headed "Accounts Receivable Dr." and "Sales Cr." These accounts are in the general ledger, and by posting this total, debits will continue to equal credits.

Review the sales journal below, which has now been posted to both subsidiary and general ledger accounts:

SALES JOURNAL   Page

Date	To Whom Sold - Account Debited	Invoice No.	PR	Accts. Rec.Dr. Sales Cr.
198- apr. 2	Best-West Sewing Machine Company	4834	✓	3096 00
9	Elaine K. Brown	4835	✓	175 00
23	Ralph Mazel & Company	4836	✓	250 00
30	Elaine K. Brown	4837	✓	200 00
30	Total			3721 00
				(13) (41)

ACCOUNTS RECEIVABLE LEDGER

Best-West Sewing Machine Company
296 South Street, Newark, NJ 07114

Date			PR	Dr.	Cr.	Dr. Bal.
198- Apr.	1	Balance	✓			300 00
	2		34	3096 00		3396 00

Elaine K. Brown
11 Harbor Road, Perth Amboy, NJ 08861

Date			PR	Dr.	Cr.	Dr. Bal.
198- Apr.	9		54	175 00		175 00
	30		54	200 00		375 00

Ralph Mazel & Company
278 Patriots Road, Morristown, NJ 07960

Date			PR	Dr.	Cr.	Dr. Bal.
198- Apr.	1	Balance	✓			400 00
	23		54	250 00		650 00

GENERAL LEDGER

Accounts Receivable   No. 13

				Dr.	Cr.	Balance	
						Dr.	Cr.
198- Apr.	1	Balance	✓			70000	
	30		54	3721 00		4421 00	

Sales   No. 41

				Dr.	Cr.	Balance	
						Dr.	Cr.
198- Apr.	30		54		3721 00		3721 00

The customers' postings are indicated by check marks (√) because these accounts have no numbers—they are arranged alphabetically. The journal total was posted to accounts No. 13 and No. 41 (Accounts Receivable and Sales).

The three-column subsidiary ledger arrangement is used also for customers' accounts. A debit increases the customer's account balance; a credit decreases the customer's account balance.

Schedule of Accounts Receivable

At the end of the month, the accuracy of postings can be proved by preparing a SCHEDULE OF ACCOUNTS RECEIVABLE. This is a listing of customers' accounts and the balance due from each. The total of the schedule should be equal to the balance of the controlling account— Accounts Receivable—which shows in *total* balance the sum of the individual subsidiary account balances.

Tri-Royal Sales Company Schedule of Accounts Receivable April 30, 198–	
Best-West Sewing Machine Company	3396 00
Elaine K. Brown	375 00
Ralph Mazel & Company	650 00
Total Accounts Receivable	4421 00

YOU SHOULD REMEMBER

A sales journal is a book of *original* entry used only to record transactions for the *sale of merchandise on account*.

The sales journal *summary entry* posting is a *debit* to *Accounts Receivable* and a *credit* to *Sales*.

The schedule of Accounts Receivable *total* equals the *balance* of the *Accounts Receivable account*.

KNOW YOUR VOCABULARY

Accounts Receivable ledger

On account

Sales journal

Schedule of Accounts Receivable

Triplicate

QUESTIONS

1. What type of transaction is recorded in a sales journal?
2. How are customers' accounts arranged in a subsidiary ledger?
3. How is the equality of general ledger debits and credits maintained when posting a sales journal?

4. How is the accuracy of the subsidiary ledger proved?
5. Why might arranging customers' accounts alphabetically be easier for a small business to manage than numbering them?
6. Why are sales invoice numbers listed in consecutive order in a sales journal?

PROBLEMS

15–1 (1) Record Mear's Department Stores sales of merchandise on account, starting with invoice No. 215:

March 2, 198–	Mrs. Edward Ardyce, $175
9,	Mr. Herman Gold, $96.50
16,	Ms. Eliza Fisher, $107.30
23,	Mrs. Edward Ardyce, $62.45
30,	Ms. Eliza Fisher, $29.50

(2) Post to the subsidiary ledger.
(3) Summarize the sales journal at the end of the month, and post to the general ledger.
(4) Prepare a schedule of accounts receivable.

(1) and (3) **SALES JOURNAL** Page 31

Date	To Whom Sold – Account Debited	Invoice No.	PR	Acct. Rec. Dr. Sales Cr.

ACCOUNTS RECEIVABLE LEDGER

(2)

Mrs. Edward Ardyce
305 Riverview Terrace, Cincinnati, OH 45204

Date			PR	Dr.	Cr.	Dr. Bal.

Ms. Eliza Fisher
851 Clarkfield Street, Cincinnati, OH 45201

Mr. Herman Gold
79 Willowbrook Drive, Cincinnati, OH 45202

Date			PR	Dr.	Cr.	Dr. Bal.
198-mar.	1	Balance	✓			258 60

GENERAL LEDGER

Accounts Receivable

(3)   No. *13*

Date			PR	Dr.	Cr.	Balance Dr.	Cr.
198– Mar 2	Balance		✓			25860	

Sales   No. *41*

			Dr.	Cr.	Balance Dr.	Cr.

(4)

Mears Department Store
Schedule of Accounts Receivable
March 31, 198—

15–2   (1)   Record the following sales of merchandise on account, starting with invoice No. 328:

April 2, 198–	Mrs. Fay Wilamowski, $47.50
6,	Ms. Shirley Callahan, $36.95
9,	Mr. William Witt, $49.25
13,	Ms. Shirley Callahan, $107.65
16,	Mrs. Marjorie Intrator, $76.80
20,	Mrs. Fay Wilamowski, $52.90
23,	Mr. William Witt, $59.20
27,	Mrs. Marjorie Intrator, $67.75
30,	Ms. Shirley Callahan, $87.00

(2)   Post to the subsidiary ledger.

(3)   Summarize the sales journal at the end of the month, and post to the general ledger.

(4)   Prepare a schedule of accounts receivable.

(1) and (3)   SALES JOURNAL   Page

Date	To Whom Sold - Account Debited	Invoice No.	PR	Acct. Rec. Dr. Sales Cr.

ACCOUNTS RECEIVABLE LEDGER

2)

Ms. Shirley Callahan
186 Mineola Boulevard, Mineola, NY 11501

Date			PR	Dr.	Cr.	Dr. Bal.
198– apr. 1	Balance		✓			45 00

Mrs. Marjorie Intrator
91 Bryn Mawr, New Hyde Park, NY 11501

Mrs. Fay Wilamowski
451 Cornell Drive, Hicksville, NY 11803

Date			PR	Dr.	Cr.	Dr. Bal.
198– apr. 1	Balance		✓			65 30

Mr. William Witt
264 Emory Road, Mineola, NY 11501

Date			PR	Dr.	Cr.	Dr. Bal.
198– apr. 1	Balance		✓			95 00

GENERAL LEDGER

Accounts Receivable   No. 13

(3)

			Dr.	Cr.	Balance Dr.	Cr.
198-apr. 1	Balance	✓			205 30	

Sales   No. 41

			Dr.	Cr.	Balance Dr.	Cr.

(4)   *Winslow's Emporium*
          Schedule of Accounts Receivable
               April 30, 198-

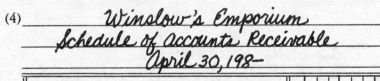

THINK IT OVER

At last count, Lacy's Department Store had approximately 110,000 charge customers. Billing procedures are now fully automated, replacing hand operation. Exactly what has been accomplished (in bookkeeping terms) by the change?

   Marshall & Kahn, a neighborhood specialty shop, is considering a change from a one-journal (general journal) bookkeeping/accounting system to using several special journals. What recommendations might be made to help in reaching a decision?

CHAPTER 16
CASH RECEIPTS JOURNAL

Receiving cash from customers is another frequent transaction. Cash is received when a cash sale is made, or when it is received from a customer ON ACCOUNT for an outstanding balance due on a credit sale. Cash is also received when borrowed, whether from a bank or an individual. In each of these transactions, the cash is in the form of either currency or a check.

In each transaction, the result is an increase in the asset cash. Therefore, an entry must be made in which cash is debited. The corresponding credit indicates the source of the cash received. A typical *general journal* entry for a cash receipt follows:

198–				
Apr.	17	Cash	7500	
		Accounts Rec./Alan Bergstrom		7500
		to Apply on Account		

Purpose of Cash Receipts Journal

General journal entries such as these require postings to all accounts—Cash Debit, Accounts Receivable Credit (in the general ledger), and Alan Bergstrom's account credit (in the subsidiary ledger). It is advisable, therefore, to use a special CASH RECEIPTS JOURNAL, which will involve less frequent and fewer postings and still keep customers' accounts up to date.

The same entry as shown above has been recorded in Betty Chan's special cash receipts journal, along with other typical cash receipts transactions:

CASH RECEIPTS JOURNAL   Page 3

Date	Account Credited	PR	General Cr.	Accts. Rec. Cr.	Cash Dr.
198- Apr. 2	Gordon Robbins			5000	5000
7	Betty Chan, Capital		250000		250000
17	Alan Bergstrom			7500	7500
19	Union National Bank		100000		100000
25	Mabel Johnson			10000	10000
30	Equipment		30000		30000

Posting to Accounts

Note that there is a special column for the controlling account—Accounts Receivable Cr. Postings are needed for all accounts credited, and are listed in the General Cr. and Accounts Receivable Cr. columns. Column totals, however, are *posted only at the end of the month*, when the journal is summarized. The columns that have identifiable account title headings are posted as indicated—Accounts Receivable Cr. (13) and Cash Dr. (11). The General Cr. column total is not posted and checked (√) because there is no *single* general ledger account for that total. Furthermore, the individual accounts listed as credited will have been posted.

Summarizing the Cash Receipts Journal

Betty Chan's journal now follows, posted and summarized:

CASH RECEIPTS JOURNAL   Page 3

Date	Account Credited	PR	General Cr.	Accts. Rec. Cr.	Cash Dr.
198- Apr. 2	Gordon Robbins	√		5000	500
7	Betty Chan, Capital	31	250000		25000
17	Alan Bergstrom	√		7500	750
19	Union National Bank	22	100000		10000
25	Mabel Johnson	√		10000	1000
30	Equipment	15	30000		3000
30	Totals		380000	22500	40250
			(√)	(13)	(11)

First, the columns were pencil footed; debit totals equal credit totals. Then they were written in ink, and the journal was double ruled. The General Dr. column is always checkmarked, and the special column totals have been posted to the accounts identified in their headings. The postings to customers' accounts and the Cash and Accounts Receivable accounts follow (General Cr. column account postings are not illustrated here):

GENERAL LEDGER

Cash   No. 11

198–				Dr.	Cr.	Balance Dr.	Balance Cr.
apr.	1	Balance	✓			78000	
	30		CR3	402500		480500	
	30		CD4		300000	180500	

Accounts Receivable   No. 13

198–			PR	Dr.	Cr.	Balance Dr.	Balance Cr.
apr.	1	Balance	✓			30000	
	30		S5	120000		150000	
	30		CR3		22500	127500	

ACCOUNTS RECEIVABLE LEDGER

Alan Bergstrom
142 Overlook Drive, Minneapolis, MN 55402

Date			PR	Dr.	Cr.	Dr. Bal.
198– Apr. 7			S5	175 00		175 0
17			CR3		75 00	100 0
24			S5	500 00		600 0

Mabel Johnson
7103 River Road, St. Paul, MN 55101

Date			PR	Dr.	Cr.	Dr. Bal.
198– Apr. 1		Balance	✓			100 0
15			S5	220 00		320 0
25			CR3		100 00	220 0

Gordon Robbins
3216 Twin Oaks Avenue, Minneapolis, MN 55407

Date			PR	Dr.	Cr.	Dr. Bal.
198– Apr. 1		Balance	✓			200 0
2			CR3		50 00	150 0
22			S5	305 00		405 0

Schedule of Accounts Receivable

At the end of the month, Betty Chan's schedule of accounts receivable is taken to prove the accuracy of the subsidiary ledger:

Betty Chan Schedule of Accounts Receivable April 30, 198–		
Alan Bergstrom		600 00
Mabel Johnson		220 00
Gordon Robbins		455 00
Total Accounts Receivable		1 275 00

The balance of the controlling account, Accounts Receivable, is also $1,275. Since the balance in the controlling account equals the total of the subsidiary ledger, the accounts receivable ledger has been "proved."

Expanding the Journal

Any cash receipts journal may be expanded to include four or more columns, depending on the needs of the business. For example, if many *cash sales* of merchandise occur, a special column—Sales Cr.—can be included. If this column is used, it is necessary to checkmark (√) the posting reference column; *no posting is needed for each cash sales entry*, inasmuch as the column total will be posted, along with all other *special column totals*, *at the end of the month*. Examine these entries in a four-column cash receipts journal:

Date	Account Debited	PR	General Cr.	Accts. Rec Cr.	Sales Cr.	Cash Cr.
98– May 3	H. L. Wicker			100 00		100 00
7	Sales	√			500 00	500 00
10	Mrs. D. Ginsburg			95 00		95 00
14	Sales	√			625 00	625 00
17	Lawrence Evans, Cap.		4000 00			4000 00
24	Sales	√			595 00	595 00
31	Sales	√			850 00	850 00
31	Totals		4000 00	195 00	2570 00	6765 00
			(√)	(√)	(√)	(√)

The bookkeeping/accounting clerk can easily see which items need to be posted, and which do not. Those that are checked *will not be posted*; items appearing in the *General Cr. and Accounts Receivable Cr. columns will be posted* periodically to the accounts identified in the Account Debited column. The *special column totals*—Accounts Receivable Cr., Sales Cr., and Cash Dr.—*will be posted* at the end of the month.

Source Documents for Cash Receipts

The cash receipts journal is a book of original entry, used exclusively for entries that result in cash debits—to increase the amount of cash. As with all entries, a source document is prepared for each cash receipt transaction; this may be a copy of a hand-prepared cash sales slip or a cash register DETAIL AUDIT TAPE, which accumulates a total of the cash register activity for each salesperson.

> **YOU SHOULD REMEMBER**
>
> Customers' account balances should be kept up to date by frequent (daily or monthly) posting.
>
> Source documents are *business forms* that serve as *evidence of every transaction*, such as invoices (one copy is evidence of a sale on account, a duplicate copy is evidence of a purchase on account) and detail audit tapes.

KNOW YOUR VOCABULARY

Cash receipts journal   On account

Detail audit tape

QUESTIONS

1. What type of transaction is exclusively entered in a cash receipts journal?
2. What justifies the use of a special column in a cash receipts journal?
3. How are postings to subsidiary ledger accounts from the cash receipts journal indicated?
4. When does a check mark indicate a posting reference?
5. When does a check mark indicate that an item is not to be posted?
6. How is the accuracy of the accounts receivable ledger proved?

PROBLEMS

16–1 Raul Garcia, owner of the Rose of Texas Specialty Gift Shop, uses a four-column cash receipts journal. Subtotals are indicated in pencil for the first 3 weeks' entries.

   (1) Continue by recording the following entries for the cash receipts transactions for the remainder of the month:

     April 23, Garcia invested an additional $2,000 cash in his business
          24, Borrowed $2,500 from Lone Star Bank; received a check for that amount
          25, Received $85 from J. R. Dallas on account

26, Received $60 from Margo Chase on account
27, Sold old office typewriter (equipment) for $95 cash
28, Received $75 from Frances Lima on account
29, Cash sales for the week amounted to $1,765

(2) Summarize the journal at the end of the month. Checkmark all items *not to be posted* separately.

(3) Post the summary entry only.

(1) and (2)

CASH RECEIPTS JOURNAL   Page 6

Date	Accts. Cr.	PR	General Cr.	Accts. Rec. Cr.	Sales Cr.	Cash Dr.
198– apr. 23			750 00	1435 00	5976 00	8161 00

GENERAL LEDGER

Cash   No. 11

Date		PR	Dr.	Cr.	Balance Dr.	Cr.
148– apr. 1	Balance	√			1935 00	

Accounts Receivable   No. 13

Date		PR	Dr.	Cr.	Balance Dr.	Cr.
148– apr. 1	Balance	√			1728 50	

Sales   No. 41

Date		PR	Dr.	Cr.	Balance Dr.	Cr.
198– mar. 31		S4		3500 00		3500 00
31		CR5		6250 00		9750 00
31		J3	9750 00			

16–2 Pat Norrell is a wholesaler who sells beauty shop supplies to barber shops and beauty salons. She uses a sales journal to record all sales of merchandise on account. She uses a four-column cash receipts journal with a sales credit column for cash sales made to customers to whom she sells merchandise for cash.

(1)   Enter the following transactions for the month, starting with invoice No. 7156:

May 1, Sold merchandise on account:
      Willow's Beauty Shoppe, $465
      Lee's Unisex, $395
  7, Cash sales for week, $252.50
 10, Received $200 from Goddess of Love
 12, Sold merchandise on account:
      Goddess of Love, $268.50
      Jayne's Curls & Waves, $175
 14, Cash sales for week, $307.25
 15, Invested an additional $3,000 cash
 17, Sold merchandise on account:
      Willow's Beauty Shoppe, $192
 19, Received $395 from Lee's Unisex
 21, Cash sales for week, $296.80
 25, Received $265 from Willow's Beauty Shoppe on account
 28, Cash sales for week, $319.90
 29, Sold merchandise on account:
      Jayne's Curls & Waves, $225
      Lee's Unisex, $315.20
 31, Cash sales for 3 days, $191.40

(2)   Post current entries on a *weekly basis*, posting first the sales journal, then the cash receipts journal.

(3)   Summarize the journals; post totals from the sales journal first, then the cash receipts journal.

(4)   Prepare a schedule of accounts receivable.

(1)   **SALES JOURNAL**   Page

Date	To Whom Sold - Account Debited	Invoice No.	PR	Acct. Rec. D Sales Cr.

CASH RECEIPTS JOURNAL   Page 6

Date	Account Credited	PR	General Cr.	Accts. Rec. Cr.	Sales Cr.	Cash Dr.

ACCOUNTS RECEIVABLE LEDGER

(2) and (3)

Goddess of Love
110 Chemung Avenue, Binghamton, NY 13901

Date		PR	Dr.	Cr.	Dr. Bal.
198— May 1	Balance	✓			2000

Jayne's Curls & Waves
39 Tompkins Avenue, Cortland, NY 13045

Lee's Unisex
451 College Heights Road, Ithaca, NY 14850

Willow's Beauty Shoppe
58 Twain Boulevard, Elmira, NY 14901

GENERAL LEDGER

3)

Cash

Page 11

Date			PR	Dr.	Cr.	Balance Dr.	Cr.
198– may 1	Balance		✓			1078 50	

Accounts Receivable

No. 13

198– may 1	Balance		✓			200 00	

Pat Norrell, Capital

No. 31

198– may 1	Balance		✓				2500000

Sales

No. 41

(4)

CHAPTER 17

GENERAL JOURNAL, FOUR-COLUMN FORMAT

There are several reasons why customers may return merchandise that was sold to them. It may be damaged, the wrong size, the wrong color, or otherwise unsatisfactory. In other cases, customers may retain possession of the merchandise but receive a reduction in the selling price.

Sales Returns and Allowances, and Purchases Returns and Allowances

In either case, a new account is involved in each of these transactions—either SALES RETURNS AND ALLOWANCES or PURCHASES RETURNS AND ALLOWANCES. A *general journal* entry illustrating the first of these follows:

198-						
May 23	Sales Returns and Allowances	44		25 75		
	Accounts Receivable/	✓			25 75	
	Judith Falkin					
	Credit Memo No. 135					

Posting references are given to show how this is handled. Because Sales Returns and Allowances represent decreases in Sales, the special numbering sequence for such VALUATION ACCOUNTS is indicated by the use of a decimal figure, as account No. 41.1. (Purchases Returns and Allowances would be account No. 51.1, which indicates decreases in Purchases.) Accounts Receivable was posted to account No. 13, and Judith Falkin was posted (√) to a subsidiary ledger account.

Source Documents

The source document for such an entry is a CREDIT MEMORANDUM, a form that is similar in appearance to the original invoice but has the words "Credit Memorandum" printed at the top and is often printed on pink paper. A copy is given to the customer (the buyer) who returns merchandise and/or is being given an allowance (by the seller).

Note the use of the diagonal line in the Posting Reference column for the credit part of this entry. Both accounts are posted—one to a general ledger account, and one to a subsidiary ledger account.

Examine carefully how the same entry is recorded in a *four-column general journal*, using columns for controlling accounts: Accts. Pay. Dr. and Accts. Rec. Cr.

GENERAL JOURNAL   Page____

Accts. Pay. Dr.	General Dr.	Date		PR	General Cr.	Accts. Rec. Cr.
	25 75	198- May 23	Sales Returns and Allowances	41.1		
			Judith Falkin	√		25 75
			Credit Memo No. 135			

Only two postings are needed for this entry—Sales Returns and Allowances and Judith Falkin. At the end of the month, the journal is summarized. The totals for the General Dr. and General Cr. columns are checkmarked, and the special columns are posted to the accounts indicated in their headings. Compare this to the entry on page 159.

A four-column general journal with typical entries follows. Explanations are given below the journal.

Accts., Pay. Dr.	General Dr.	Date		PR	General Cr.	Accts. Rec. Cr.
	50 00	198- May 2	Priscilla Deutsch			
			Priscilla Deitch		50 00	
			Correct Posting Error 4/18/8-			
	260 00	9	Martin Hande, Drawing			
			Purchases		260 00	
			Merchandise for Personal Use			
	25 75	23	Sales Returns and Allowances			
			Judith Falkin			25 75
			Credit Memo No. 135			
75 00		25	Kevin Sullivan & Company			
			Purchases Returns and		75 00	
			Allowances			
			Debit Memo No. 52			
	275 00	29	Equipment			
			Martin Hande, Capital		275 00	
			Transferred Typewriter to			
			Business			
75 00	610 75	31	Totals		660 00	25 75
( )	(✓)				(✓)	( )

Correcting Errors in Ledger Postings

On May 2, a CORRECTING ENTRY was made. Because of similarity in names, a posting error was made last month. A charge to Priscilla Deutsch for merchandise sold on account was posted to Priscilla Deitch. It appears as a debit in the wrong account. It should be in the Deutsch account. This entry corrects the error and can be entered in the General Dr. and General Cr. columns, inasmuch as it *does not affect* the Accounts Receivable account.

On May 9, the owner, Martin Hande, withdrew *merchandise* for personal use. Merchandise *purchased* for resale to customers is, therefore, reduced by the cost price of whatever was withdrawn. Since purchases are debits, *withdrawals of merchandise are credits to the Purchases account.*

On May 23, a charge customer, Judith Falkin, returned damaged merchandise for credit. Credit memorandum No. 135 was completed, and a copy (source document) used for this entry, which *decreases the customer's account balance.* Since this amount is entered in the controlling account column, it will also decrease that account balance when the column total is posted at the end of the month.

On May 25, the owner returned merchandise purchased on account to a creditor, Kevin Sullivan & Company. This is a DEBIT MEMORANDUM, a copy of the original memorandum completed by the seller. This entry *decreases the balance owed to the creditor,* as well as the controlling account when the column total is posted at the end of the month.

On May 29, the owner transferred to his business a typewriter formerly used at home. This increases his owner's equity, as any investment would.

At the end of the month, the general journal summary entry shows that the General Dr. and General Cr. column totals are checkmarked. They are not to be posted. The individual items in these two columns will be posted daily (or as soon as possible) during the month. The special account column totals will be posted to accounts identified in their headings. In this way, the controlling accounts—Accounts Receivable and Accounts Payable—will continue to show in totals what individual customers' and creditors' accounts show in their respective subsidiary ledgers.

Statement of Account

Periodically—at the end of each month, or at set dates during the month—the seller of merchandise sends each charge customer a STATEMENT OF ACCOUNT. This "bill" may be in the form of punched cards or of a detailed list of all transactions. Illustrated below is a statement sent by a seller to one of its charge customers:

BOSTON WHOLESALE SUPPLY COMPANY
1219 Beacon Street
Boston, MA 02105

May 31   198-

Mr. James Wolff
351 Tremont Street
Brighton, MA 02135

		CHARGES		
May 4	8-	Sales Slip No. 408	25 00	
22	8-	Sales Slip No. 573	40 00	65 00
		PAYMENTS/RETURNS		
May 28	8-	Check No. 79	25 00	
28	8-	Credit Memo No. 91	15 00	40 00
		Balance Due		25 00

The charges are debit postings to this customer's account. The payment/returns are credit postings. The balance due is the same as the last balance in the customer's account. Occasionally a *customer may overpay* an account (the balance due). Should this happen, there would be a *credit balance* in the customer's account, an account that normally has a debit balance. (If a creditor's account is overpaid, there would be a *debit balance* in an account that normally has a credit balance.)

A *cash refund or allowance* may be given to a *customer*. This is a cash disbursements journal entry in which Sales Returns and Allowances is debited and Cash is credited. If the *buyer* is given the cash refund or allowance, a cash receipts journal entry will be made in which Purchases Returns and Allowances is credited and Cash is debited.

YOU SHOULD REMEMBER

A four-column general journal includes special columns for any *debits* to *Accounts Payable* and any *credits* to *Accounts Receivable*.

General debit and credit *column totals* are *checkmarked* to indicate that those *totals are not to be posted*.

Valuation accounts (returns and allowance accounts) *reduce* the balance of the account to which they are "related."

KNOW YOUR VOCABULARY

Correcting entry

Credit memorandum

Debit memorandum

Purchases returns and allowances

Sales returns and allowances

Statement of account

Valuation account

QUESTIONS

1. What are the column headings of a four-column general journal?
2. What is the posting procedure from a four-column general journal?
3. What kinds of entries are recorded in a general journal?
4. Henry Jones sold merchandise to Claire Smith on account. Part of it is returned for credit. What entry is made in Jones's records? What entry is made in Smith's records?
5. What is the source document for Jones's entry? What is the source document for Smith's entry?
6. What information is reported in a customer's statement of account?

PROBLEMS

17–1 (1) Record the following entries on journal page 7 for Philip Scheiber, the owner of Scheiber's Music Emporium:

> May 2, Allowed Jane McDonald $35 credit for damaged merchandise; credit memo No. 18
>
> 5, Correct $65 posting error for sale on account to Hedy Nachtigal, posted incorrectly to Netty Nachtigal
>
> 9, Received $100 allowance on merchandise purchased from Baldwin Piano Company; debit memo No. 53
>
> 15, Took a $95 guitar as a gift for nephew
>
> 22, Allowed Alice Glaser $80 credit for return of damaged merchandise; credit memo No. 19
>
> 29, Transferred a $185 desk from home to the business office

(2) Summarize the general journal and indicate by a check mark any column total *not to be posted*.

Accts.Pay. Dr.	General Dr.	Date		PR	General Cr.	Accts. Rec. Cr.

17–2 Record the following entries on journal page 5 for Carol Dambroff, owner of Carol's Quality Draperies:

May 3, Returned to Home Decorator's Corp. $160 worth of poor quality merchandise purchased on account last month; debit memo No. AR-51

10, Paid $38 cash refund to customer who returned merchandise; check No. 326

17, Granted a $77 credit to Mrs. Robin Muir for merchandise returned; credit memo No. 39

24, Received a $50 cash refund for wrong-size merchandise paid for last month

28, Correct $140 posting error for purchase on account from C. Wilton Fabric Company, credited incorrectly to Carl Walton Furniture Company's account

GENERAL JOURNAL   Page 5

Accts. Pay Dr.	General Dr.		Date		PR	General Cr.	Accts. Rec. Cr.

CASH RECEIPTS JOURNAL   Page 12

Date	Acct. Cr.	PR	Gen. Cr.	Acct. Rec. Cr.	Sales Cr.	Cash Dr.

CASH DISBURSEMENTS JOURNAL   Page 11

Date	Acct. Dr.	Ck. No.	PR	Gen. Dr.	Acct. Pay. Dr.	Purch. Dr.	Cash Cr.

17–3   Below is the ledger account for a customer, Pearl Nathanson, of Hudson's Department
Store. Prepare a statement of account, dated May 20.

Ms. Pearl Nathanson
972 Riverside Dr.
St. Louis, MO 63104

198– May						
1		S3		60 00		60 00
5		S4		75 00		135 00
12		J2			35 00	100 00
15		CR5			20 00	75 00
18		S5		45 00		120 00

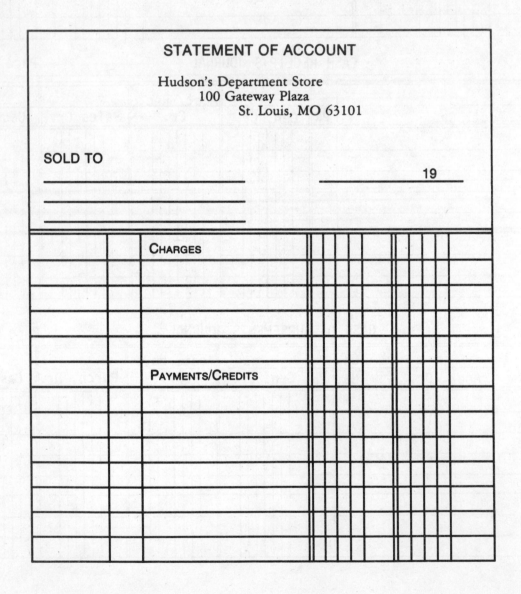

STATEMENT OF ACCOUNT

Hudson's Department Store
100 Gateway Plaza
St. Louis, MO 63101

SOLD TO

_____   _____ 19___

_____

_____

		CHARGES			
		PAYMENTS/CREDITS			

17–4 Comprehensive Five-Journal Problem.

Edward Shaw owns and operates a retail jewelry business. He uses special journals for

(1) sales of merchandise on account,
(2) purchases of merchandise on account,
(3) cash disbursements,
(4) cash receipts, and
(5) all other transactions are recorded in a general journal.

(1) Record the following transactions in the appropriate journals:

May 1, 198–	Paid Winslow Jewelers $465; check No. 392
	Paid rent for month $450; check No. 393
3,	Received cash on account from:
	Marc Green, $150
	Gian Polidoro, $95
4,	Sold merchandise on account to:
	Antonio Lorenzo, $300; invoice No. B192
	Edward Grabczak, $250; invoice No. B193
8,	Correct $35 posting error for supplies incorrectly posted to Equipment
11,	Sold merchandise on account to Marc Green, $275; invoice No. B194
13,	Withdrew $500 *cash* for personal use; check No. 394
14,	Paid clerks' salaries, $300; check No. 395
17,	Purchased merchandise on account:
	Schmidt & Brendle, $375
	Winston Jewelers, $1,200
22,	Received cash on account from:
	Antonio Lorenzo, $50
	Edward Grabczak, $125
24,	Allowed $75 credit to Marc Green for damaged merchandise; credit memo No. 35
28,	Paid Schmidt & Brendle $375; check No. 396
29,	Paid $40 refund to customer for returned merchandise; check No. 397
31,	Cash sales to date, $2,740
31,	Took a $200 ring home as gift for wife

(2) Summarize all journals. Checkmark any items, current entries and totals, that are not to be posted.

PURCHASES JOURNAL   Page *10*

Date		Account Credited		Inv. No.	PR	Purchases Dr. Acct. Pay. Cr.

SALES JOURNAL   Page 14

Date		Account Debited		PR	Acct. Rec. Dr Sales Cr.

CASH RECEIPTS JOURNAL   Page 19

Date			PR	Gen. Cr.	Acct. Rec. Cr	Sales Cr.	Cash Dr.
198– May	1	Balance on hand $1,500	✓				

CASH DISBURSEMENTS JOURNAL

Date		Ck. No.	PR	Gen. Dr.	Acct. Pay. Dr.	Purch. Dr.	Cash Cr.

GENERAL JOURNAL Page 5

Acct. Pay. Dr.	Gen. Dr.	Date		PR	Gen. Cr.	Acct. Rec. Cr.

CHAPTER

EIGHT-COLUMN WORK SHEET

Up to this point in a merchandising business, the bookkeeping/accounting cycle has followed these steps:

(1) A business transaction occurs, resulting in a document—an invoice (sales and purchases), a check, a debit or credit memorandum, and so on.

(2) The transaction is journalized.

(3) The journal entry is posted to ledger accounts; summary entries are posted.

Trial Balance

To complete all the work required in the cycle, a trial balance is prepared. This may be a separate, formal statement, or it may be completed as the first two columns of an EIGHT-COLUMN WORK SHEET. This trial balance is a listing of *all general ledger accounts*, including those that do not have balances—Revenue and Expense Summary, and certain expenses as well.

Adjusting Entries

An eight-column work sheet provides columnar space to adjust the accounts that have not been kept up to date. Some changes in account balances were not recorded in the journals, and therefore not posted to accounts. It is now necessary to bring them up to date. This is accomplished by entering ADJUSTMENTS in the special work sheet columns.

MERCHANDISE INVENTORY

In a merchandising business, one of the major assets is the MERCHANDISE INVENTORY. As merchandise is purchased and sold, however, no entries are made to the Merchandise Inventory account. All purchases are debits to the Purchases account; all sales are credits to the Sales account. However, the cost value (or possibly some other basis for evaluating merchandise) is an asset value. At the end of each fiscal period, the new, closing, or ending inventory is taken. The beginning, or opening, inventory (last fiscal period's ending inventory) has undoubtedly been sold, and is, therefore, part of the revenue and expense for the fiscal period. To record this change in inventory values, adjusting entries are made on the work sheet. See adjusting entry (A) in the sample work sheet on page 173, which *debits Revenue and Expense Summary* and *credits Merchandise Inventory*, using the amount of the *old, beginning inventory*. This actually "zeroes out" the Merchandise account balance. To record the new, ending inventory, adjusting entry (B) *debits Merchandise Inventory* and *credits Revenue and Expense Summary*, using the amount of the inventory at the *end of the fiscal period*.

SUPPLIES

The trial balance lists the SUPPLIES account at its beginning balance, plus any supplies acquired during the fiscal period. The fact that some of these supplies may have been used during the fiscal period has not been recorded. Therefore a supplies inventory is taken to determine the value on hand at the end of the fiscal period. To find the *amount used* during that time, the ending inventory is subtracted from the account balance. The *difference is the expense* for supplies. See adjusting entry (C), which *debits Supplies Expense* and *credits Supplies* for that *difference*.

OTHER PREPAID EXPENSES

Other PREPAID EXPENSES—assets such as prepaid insurance, which become expenses by being used up in a relatively short period—are adjusted in the same way. Their respective expense accounts are debited, and the prepaid assets are credited for *the amount used* during the fiscal period.

Extending Updated Balances

Each of the amounts is extended to one of the remaining columns to complete the work sheet. Examine each account, its debits and/or credits, in the first four columns, in order to determine the updated balance or amount to be extended to one of the remaining four columns in either the Income Statement or the Balance Sheet column. Revenue and Expense Summary adjustment figures are carried to *both* Income Statement columns; each of the other account balances is extended to only one column.

Determining Net Income or Net Loss

When the extensions are completed properly, the *differences in column totals in each pair should be equal*. The amount is either a net income or a net loss for the fiscal period—*net income* if the Income Statement credit column total is greater than the debit column; *net loss* if the reverse is true.

The amount of net income is entered in each pair of columns, to be added to the smaller column total, thus giving two equal totals for each pair of columns. In the Income Statement columns, the total is entered in the debit column; in the Balance Sheet columns, it is entered in the credit column. The final equal totals are then double ruled, and the words "Net Income" are written on the proper line in the Account Title column.

Fields and Ross
Work Sheet
For Year Ended December 31, 198-

Account Title	A. N.	Trial Balance Debit	Trial Balance Credit	Adjustments Debit	Adjustments Credit	Income Statement Debit	Income Statement Credit	Balance Sheet Debit	Balance Sheet Credit
Cash	111	225000						225000	
Petty Cash	112	5000						5000	
Accounts Receivable	113	317500						317500	
Merchandise Inventory	114	1550000		(A) 1360000	(A) 1550000			1360000	
Equipment	115	1500000						1500000	
Supplies	116	139000			(C) 95000			44000	
Accounts Payable	211		205000						205000
O. Y. Fields, Capital	311		1159500						1159500
O. Y. Fields, Drawing	311.1	1200000						1200000	
B. W. Ross, Capital	312		1261000						1261000
B. W. Ross, Drawing	312.1	1200000						1200000	
Income and Expense Summary	313			(A) 1550000	(B) 1360000	1550000	1360000		
Sales	411		7600000				7600000		
Sales Returns & Allow.	411.1	175000				175000			
Purchases	511	3000000				3000000			
Purchases Returns & Allow.	511.1		58000				58000		
Advertising Expense	611	120000				120000			
Miscellaneous Expense	612	12000				12000			
Rent Expense	613	240000				240000			
Salary Expense	614	600000				600000			
Supplies Expense	615			(C) 95000		95000			
		10283500	10283500	3005000	3005000	5792000	9018000	5851500	2625500
Net Income						3226000			3226000
						9018000	9018000	5851500	5851500

Notice that the completed work sheet on page 173 is for a PARTNERSHIP, Fields and Ross. In a partnership, two or more individuals combine their investments and operate a business according to an agreement. The amounts invested, the responsibilities of the partners, and the method for sharing net income or net losses should be spelled out in detail. In that way future disagreements may be avoided.

YOU SHOULD REMEMBER

The Revenue and Expense Summary account is used to *make certain adjusting entries* (for merchandise inventory) at the end of a fiscal period.

Prepaid expenses *are assets when first acquired*, but become expenses as they are used, thus requiring an adjustment to record this change.

KNOW YOUR VOCABULARY

Adjustments (adjusting entries)   Partnership

Eight-column work sheet   Prepaid assets

Merchandise inventory

QUESTIONS

1. What are the four headings for the four pairs of columns in an eight-column work sheet?
2. How is the end-of-fiscal-period merchandise inventory determined?
3. What does the first merchandise adjusting entry (A) accomplish?
4. What does the second merchandise adjusting entry (B) accomplish?
5. How are the Balance Sheet column extended amounts determined for
   a) merchandise inventory, and
   b) prepaid expenses?
6. Why do prepaid expenses have to be adjusted at the end of a fiscal period?
7. How is a net income for the fiscal period determined?
8. How is a net loss for the fiscal period determined?

PROBLEMS

(Save your work for use in Chapters 19 and 20.)

18-1 Daniel Green's general ledger account balances are given below:

Cash	$ 1,200
Accounts Receivable	2,500
Merchandise Inventory	5,000
Equipment	6,000
Supplies	400
Accounts Payable	1,800
Daniel Green, Capital	14,200
Daniel Green, Drawing	1,500
Revenue and Expense Summary	---
Sales	6,500
Sales Returns and Allowances	250
Purchases	3,000
Purchase Returns and Allowances	150
Miscellaneous Expense	100
Rent Expense	1,200
Salary Expense	1,500
Supplies Expense	---

Complete the work sheet on page 176 for the quarter ended June 30, 198-, using the following information for adjustments:

Merchandise inventory, June 30	$5,175
Supplies on hand	$ 300

18-2 Timothy Sullivan's general ledger is given on pages 177-180. Complete the eight-column work sheet on page 181, using the following additional information:

Merchandise Inventory, Jan. 31	$3,950
Supplies on hand	$ 205
Prepaid insurance	$ 250

Account Title	A.N.	Trial Balance		Adjustments		Income Statement		Balance Sheet	
		Debit	Credit	Debit	Credit	Debit	Credit	Debit	Credit

Cash   No. 11

Date			PR	Dr.	Cr.	Balance Dr.	Balance Cr.
198– Jan. 1	Balance		✓			1500 00	
31			CR2	3650 00		5150 00	
31			CP3		1790 00	3360 00	

Accounts Receivable   No. 12

Date			PR	Dr.	Cr.	Balance Dr.	Balance Cr.
198– Jan. 1	Balance		✓			500 00	
31			S2	3200 00		3700 00	
31			CR2		150 00	3550 00	
31			J1		35 00	3515 00	

Merchandise Inventory   No. 13

Date			PR	Dr.	Cr.	Balance Dr.	Balance Cr.
198– Jan. 1	Balance		✓			3800 00	

Supplies   No. 14

Date			PR	Dr.	Cr.	Balance Dr.	Balance Cr.
198– Jan. 1	Balance		✓			275 00	
3			CP2	50 00		325 00	

Prepaid Insurance   No. 15

Date		PR	Dr.	Cr.	Balance Dr.	Balance Cr.
198– Jan. 1	Balance	✓			30000	

Accounts Payable   No. 21

Date		PR	Dr.	Cr.	Balance Dr.	Balance Cr.
198– Jan. 1	Balance	✓				100000
31		P2		120000		220000
31		CP3	40000			180000

Timothy Sullivan, Capital   No 31

Date		PR	Dr.	Cr.	Balance Dr.	Balance Cr.
198– Jan. 1	Balance	✓				537500
10		CR3		250000		787500

Timothy Sullivan, Drawing   No. 32

Date		PR	Dr.	Cr.	Balance Dr.	Balance Cr.
198– Jan. 15		CP2	15000		15000	
30		CP2	15000		30000	

Revenue and Expense Summary   No. 33

Date		PR	Dr.	Cr.	Balance Dr.	Cr.

Sales   No. 41

Date		PR	Dr.	Cr.	Balance Dr.	Cr.
198- Jan 31		S2		3200 00		3200 00
31		CR8		1000 00		4200 00

Sales-Returns and Allowances   No. 411

Date		PR	Dr.	Cr.	Balance Dr.	Cr.
198- Jan 20		J2	35 00		35 00	

Purchases   No. 51

Date		PR	Dr.	Cr.	Balance Dr.	Cr.
198- Jan 31		P2	1200 00		1200 00	
31		CP3	500 00		1700 00	

Advertising Expense   No. 61

Date		PR	Dr.	Cr.	Balance Dr.	Balance Cr.
198- Jan 3		CP2	100 00		100 00	

Insurance Expense   No. 62

Date		PR	Dr.	Cr.	Balance Dr.	Balance Cr.

Miscellaneous Expense   No. 63

Date		PR	Dr.	Cr.	Balance Dr.	Balance Cr.
198- Jan 12		CP2	25 00		25 00	
27		CP2	15 00		40 00	

Rent Expense   No. 64

Date		PR	Dr.	Cr.	Balance Dr.	Balance Cr.
198- Jan 2		CP2	400 00		400 00	

Supplies Expense   No. 65

Date		PR	Dr.	Cr.	Balance Dr.	Balance Cr.

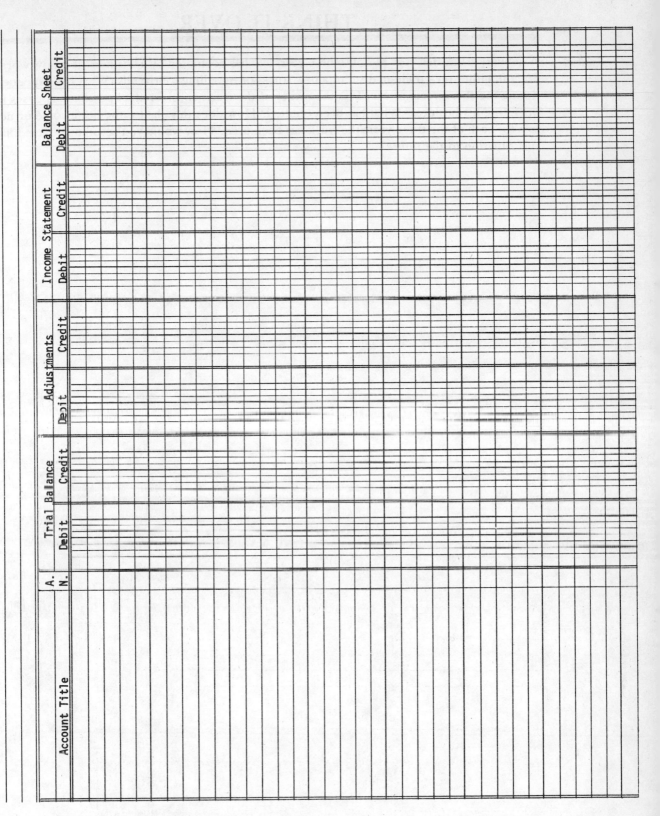

THINK IT OVER

A delivery truck that cost $12,500 three years ago has been used by a business. It is now worth $6,500, either on a trade-in deal for a new truck, or by selling it privately. What has happened during the three years of use? Has the owner of the truck considered all possible expenses in operating his business? What has been omitted? How does this change the net income or net loss for each of the three years the truck has been used? How would you recommend handling this situation in the future?

CHAPTER 19

FINANCIAL STATEMENTS

At the end of each fiscal period, financial statements are prepared to summarize the operations of a business. This information allows the owner(s) to see how profitable (or unprofitable) the business has been, to compare one fiscal period with prior periods, and to determine future courses of action. In addition, this information may be requested by banks, and by the Internal Revenue Service if tax returns are examined.

Income Statement

An INCOME STATEMENT describes the way in which a business has operated during a fiscal period. It is prepared from information on the work sheet in the special Income Statement columns. The income statement for Fields and Ross (see work sheet, page 173) follows:

Fields and Ross Income Statement For Year Ended December 31, 198—			
Income:			
Sales		7600000	
Less Sales Returns and Allowances		175000	
Net Sales			7425000
Cost of Goods Sold:			
Merchandise Inv., Jan. 1		1550000	
Purchases	30,000		
Less Purchases Returns and Allowances	580		
Net Purchases		2942000	
Merchandise Available for Sale		4492000	
Less Merchandise Inv., Dec. 31		1360000	
Cost of Goods Sold			3132000
Gross Profit on Sales			4293000
Expenses:			
Advertising Expense		170000	
Miscellaneous Expense		12000	
Rent Expense		240000	
Salary Expense		600000	
Supplies Expense		95000	
Total Expenses			1067000
Net Income			3226000

The customary three-line heading indicates the answers to WHO, WHAT, and WHEN. The statement is divided into five parts:

(1) An *income* section, listing all operating income earned during the fiscal period—sales, less sales returns and allowances.

> Sales − Sales Returns and Allowances = Net Sales

(2) A *cost of goods sold* section, which includes the following: beginning inventory, plus net purchases (purchases, less purchases returns and allowances), less ending inventory.

Beginning Inventory + Net Purchases − Ending Inventory = Cost of Goods Sold

(3) The *gross profit*, which is the difference between net sales and cost of goods sold.

Net Sales − Cost of Goods Sold = Gross Profit

(4) The *expenses* section, listing all operating expenses for the fiscal period.
(5) The *net income*, which is the difference between gross profit on sales and total expenses.

Gross Profit − Total Expenses = Net Income (or Net Loss)

In the event that total expenses exceed gross profit on sales, the result is a net loss for the fiscal period.

Briefly stated, an income statement shows

Net Sales

− Cost of Goods Sold

= Gross Profit on Sales

− Total Expenses

= Net Income (or Net Loss)

An income statement for a business owned by a single owner does not differ from one for a business owned by two or more people.

There must be an agreement as to how partners are to share any net income or net loss. If Fields and Ross in our example share equally, each partner would receive $16,130 (one half of $32,260). If partners share in any other way, this must be clearly stated in the ARTICLES OF PARTNERSHIP, the written agreement establishing the business. Assume in the case of Fields and Ross that the agreement provides for the partners to share income and losses *in the ratio* of 3 to 2 (3:2). This means that Fields would receive three fifths ($\frac{3}{5}$) or 60%, and Ross two fifths ($\frac{2}{5}$) or 40%, of any net income or any net loss.

Fields's share of the net income is, therefore, $19,356 ($\frac{3}{5}$ or 60% of $32,260), and Ross's share is $12,904 ($\frac{2}{5}$ or 40% of $32,260).

Capital Statement

This information is included in the CAPITAL STATEMENT, which shows how each partner's owner's equity changed during the fiscal period.

Fields and Ross
Capital Statement
For Year Ended December 31, 198—

A. G. Fields:			
Beginning Balance, Jan. 1		11 595 00	
Plus 3/5 of Net Income	19,356		
Less Withdrawals	12,000		
Net Increase in Capital		7 356 00	
Ending Balance, Dec. 31			18 951 00
B. W. Ross:			
Beginning Balance, Jan. 1		10 610 00	
Plus: Additional Investment	2,000		
2/5 of Net Income	12,904		
	14,904		
Less Withdrawals	12,000		
Net Increase in Capital		2 904 00	
Ending Balance, Dec. 31			13 514 00
Total Owner's Equity, Dec. 31			32 465 00

Examine the following capital statement for Lois Berlowitz, who had a loss for the fiscal period:

Lois Berlowitz
Capital Statement
For Six Months Ended June 30, 198—

Beginning Balance, Jan. 1		28 765 00
Additional Investment		2 500 00
		31 265 00
Less: Net Loss	5 200 00	
Withdrawals	6 000 00	
Total Decrease in Capital		11 200 00
Ending Balance, June 30		20 065 00

Balance Sheet

The next financial statement to be prepared is a **BALANCE SHEET**. This shows the financial condition of a business at the end of the fiscal period. The form presented below is the REPORT FORM balance sheet, listing items (assets, liabilities, and owners' equity) vertically, one under the other. Notice, however, that the fundamental bookkeeping/accounting equation is maintained and is emphasized by double-ruling *total assets* and *total liabilities plus owners' equity*.

Fields and Ross
Balance Sheet
December 31, 198-

Assets		
Cash	225000	
Petty Cash	5000	
Accounts Receivable	317500	
Merchandise Inventory	1360000	
Equipment	1500000	
Supplies	44000	
Total Assets		3451500
Liabilities		
Accounts Payable		205000
Owners' Equity		
A. H. Fields, Capital	1895100	
B. W. Ross, Capital	1351400	
Total Owners' Equity		3246500
Total Liabilities and Owners' Equity		3451500

KNOW YOUR VOCABULARY

Articles of partnership
Balance Sheet
Capital statement
Cost of goods sold

Gross profit
Income statement
Partnership
Report form balance sheet

QUESTIONS

1. What information is shown on each of the following?
   a) An income statement.
   b) A capital statement.
   c) A balance sheet.
2. How is the cost of goods sold calculated?
3. What determines whether there is a net income or a net loss for a fiscal period?
4. How does a report form balance sheet differ from an account form balance sheet?

PROBLEMS

19–1 Using the completed work sheet for Daniel Green (Problem 18–1), complete:
   1) An income statement.
   2) A capital statement (assume that Green's capital includes a $2,000 additional investment).
   3) A balance sheet.

1) _____

2)

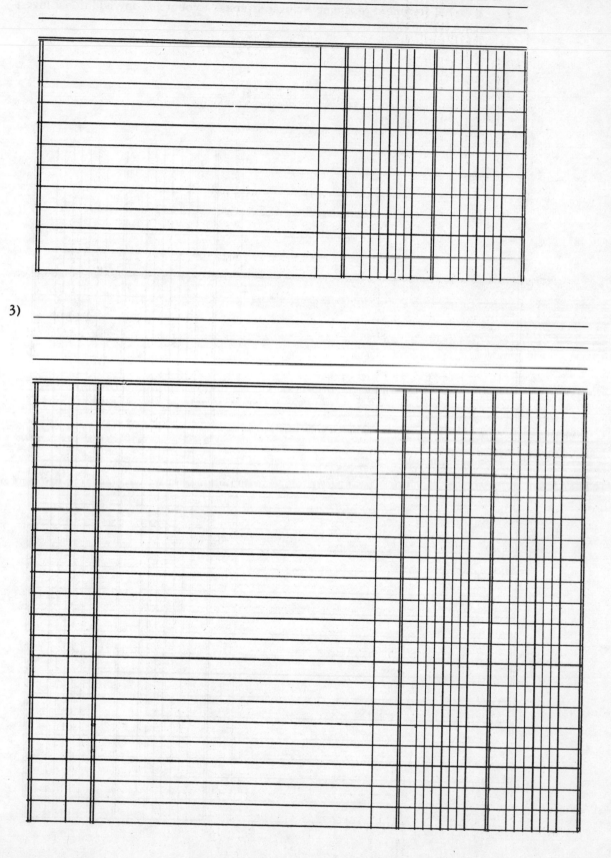

3)

19–2   Using the completed work sheet for Timothy Sullivan (Problem 18–2), complete:
1)   An income statement.
2)   A capital statement (examine Sullivan's capital account for any additional invest-ment; see pp. 178–181).
3)   A balance sheet.

1)

2)

3)

19–3 Abdullah and Pahlevi are partners who share profits and losses in the ratio of 4:3. Their general ledger account balances at the end of the year are as follows:

Cash	$ 3,625
Accounts Receivable	18,260
Merchandise Inventory, January 1	22,320
Equipment	7,500
Prepaid Insurance	500
Supplies	275
Accounts Payable	3,105
T. G. Abdullah, Capital	33,802
T. G. Abdullah, Drawing	10,000
S. H. Pahlevi, Capital	28,404
S. H. Pahlevi, Drawing	12,000
Revenue and Expense Summary	– –
Sales	51,790
Sales Returns and Allowances	2,570
Purchases	31,380
Purchases Returns and Allowances	1,529
Advertising Expense	600
Insurance Expense	– –
Rent Expense	3,600
Salary Expense	6,000
Supplies Expense	– –

Additional Information, December 31:

Merchandise Inventory	$23,195
Prepaid Insurance	$400
Supplies on Hand	$178.50

Complete the following:
1) A work sheet.
2) An income statement.
3) A capital statement (assume that Abdullah made a $5,000 additional investment during the fiscal period, which was included in his capital account balance).
4) A balance sheet.

1)

Account Title	A. N.	Trial Balance		Adjustments		Income Statement		Balance Sheet	
		Debit	Credit	Debit	Credit	Debit	Credit	Debit	Credit

(2)

(3)

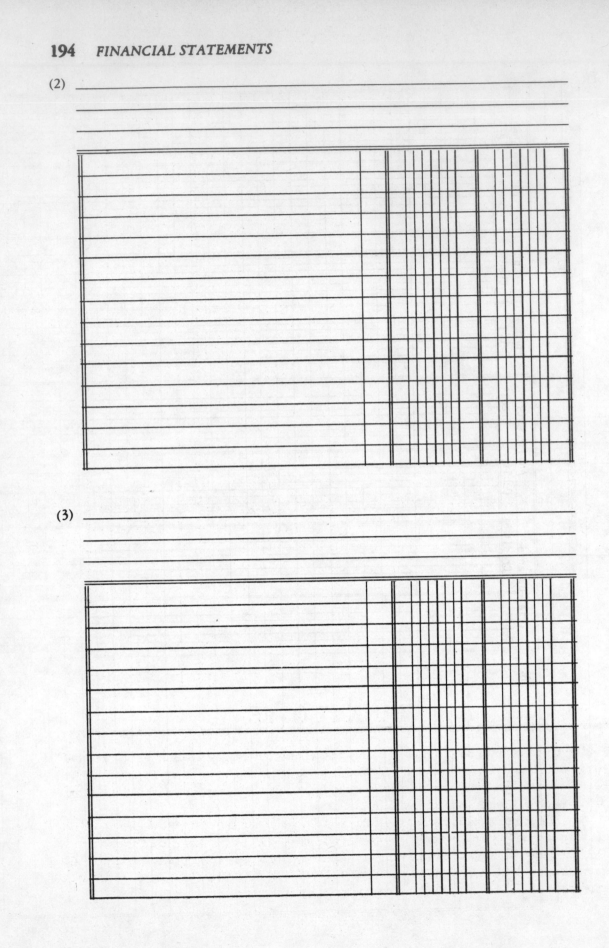

4) _____
_____
_____

THINK IT OVER

Paul Garrison believes his balance sheet does not reflect a correct end-of-fiscal-period financial condition. He is concerned because several of his charge customers (accounts receivable) have been unable to pay him amounts that are due. In past years, he has seen a similar situation: there are always some uncollectible accounts.

Does this situation affect the value of Garrison's assets? What adjustment might be made to account for an estimated loss on "bad debts" at the end of each fiscal period?

How would this adjustment affect Garrison's operating expenses if he estimates that approximately $500 may be uncollectible accounts receivable and, therefore, another operating expense?

CHAPTER

ADJUSTING AND CLOSING THE GENERAL LEDGER

In Chapters 18 and 19, work sheets with adjustments were completed, and certain accounts were brought up to date. These ADJUSTING ENTRIES reflected the changes that had taken place but had not been recorded in the actual accounts. *General ledger accounts* must now be brought up to date so that these changes become part of the permanent bookkeeping/accounting records.

Adjusting Accounts

Examine the Adjustments columns of the work sheet for Fields and Ross, page 174. Entries, with debits and credits identified by letters A, B, and C, pair off each adjustment. These are

197

recorded in a general journal (using the General Dr. and General Cr. columns of a four-column general journal). The illustration below shows these adjusting entries *posted* to general ledger accounts.

GENERAL JOURNAL   Page 4

Accts. Pay. Dr.	General Dr.	Date		PR	General Cr.	Accts. Rec. Cr.
		198-	Adjusting Entries			
	1550000	Dec. 31	Revenue and Expense Summary	313		
			Merchandise Inventory	114	1550000	
	1360000	31	Merchandise Inventory	114		
			Revenue and Expense Summary	313	1360000	
	95000	31	Supplies Expense	615		
			Supplies	116	95000	

GENERAL LEDGER

Merchandise Inventory   No. 114

Date		PR	Dr.	Cr.	Balance Dr.	Cr.
198- Jan. 1	Balance	✓			1550000	
Dec. 31		J4		1550000	—	
31		J4	1360000		1360000	

Supplies   No. 116

Date		PR	Dr.	Cr.	Balance Dr.	Cr.
198- Jan. 1	Balance	✓			50000	
May 15		CP3	60000		110000	
Nov. 3		CP8	29000		139000	
Dec. 31		J4		95000	44000	

Revenue and Expense Summary   No. 313

Date		PR	Dr.	Cr.	Balance Dr.	Balance Cr.
198- Dec. 31		J4	1550000		1550000	
31		J4		1360000	190000	

Supplies Expense   No. 615

Date		PR	Dr.	Cr.	Balance Dr.	Balance Cr.
198- Dec. 31		J4	95000		95000	

The ledger Posting Reference column indicates postings from general journal page 4 (J4). These accounts—Merchandise Inventory, Supplies, and Supplies Expense—are now up to date.

Closing Accounts

The next step at the end of the fiscal period is the closing procedure. Examine once again the Fields and Ross work sheet, page 174. The accounts listed in the Income Statement columns— all *revenue, cost, and expense accounts*, and the *Revenue and Expense Summary account*—and, in the Balance Sheet debit column, the *drawing accounts* are temporary accounts that are to be closed or "zeroed out." The information they show is for one fiscal period only and does not carry over to succeeding periods. CLOSING ENTRIES will close these temporary accounts.

First, close the accounts listed in the Income Statement credit column. They are *debited* to "zero out," and their total is *credited* to Revenue and Expense Summary.

Second, close the accounts listed in the Income Statement debit column. They are *credited* to "zero out," and their total is *debited* to Revenue and Expense Summary.

Third, close the Revenue and Expense Summary account. The amount of *net income* is *debited* to Revenue and Expense Summary to "zero out" and is *credited* to the owners' capital accounts. (Had there been a *net loss*, the debits and credits would have been reversed.)

Fourth, close the drawing accounts. Owners' capital accounts are *debited*, and their drawing accounts are *credited* to "zero out."

Closing entries continue in the general journal, immediately following the adjusting entries:

			Closing Entries		
7600000		31	*Sales*		
58000			*Purchases Returns and Allcos.*		
			Revenue and Expense Summary	7658000	
4242000		31	*Revenue and Expense Summary*		
			Sales Returns and Allowances	175000	
			Purchases	3000000	
			Advertising Expense	120000	
			Miscellaneous Expense	12000	
			Rent Expense	240000	
			Salary Expense	600000	
			Supplies Expense	95000	
3226000		31	*Revenue and Expense Summary*		
			A. G. Fields, Capital	1935600	
			B. W. Ross, Capital	1290400	
1200000		31	*A. G. Fields, Capital*		
1200000			*B. W. Ross, Capital*		
			A. G. Fields, Drawing	1200000	
			B. W. Ross, Drawing	1200000	

These entries are then posted to the general ledger.

Post-Closing Trial Balance

To prove that the adjusting and closing work has been completed correctly, a last POST-CLOSING TRIAL BALANCE is taken. The accounts that are open at this point will have balances that carry over to succeeding fiscal periods. These are balance sheet accounts—*assets*, *liabilities*, and *capital*. Below is the post-closing trial balance for Fields and Ross. (If a complete general ledger had been illustrated here, all of these account balances would now be apparent, and they would be the source of the information listed.)

Fields and Ross Post-closing Trial Balance December 31, 198-		
Cash	2250 00	
Petty Cash	50 00	
Accounts Receivable	3175 00	
Merchandise Inventory	13600 00	
Equipment	15000 00	
Supplies	440 00	
Accounts Payable		2050 00
A. G. Fields, Capital		18951 00
B. W. Ross, Capital		13514 00
	34515 00	34515 00

YOU SHOULD REMEMBER

Adjusting and closing entries are not transactions; they are the bookkeeper's way of first *bringing accounts up to date, and then zeroing out income, cost, expense and drawing account balances* at the end of each fiscal period.

A post-closing trial balance lists only accounts which have *balances that carry over to the succeeding fiscal period.*

KNOW YOUR VOCABULARY

Adjusting entry   Post-closing trial balance
Closing Entry

QUESTIONS

1. How are debits and credits for each adjustment shown on the work sheet?
2. Why is it necessary to journalize and post adjusting entries, inasmuch as they are included on the work sheet?
3. Which columns of the work sheet contain information needed for journalizing closing entries?
4. What does the first closing entry accomplish?
5. What does the second closing entry accomplish?
6. What is the third closing entry when there has been a net income for the fiscal period? A net loss for the fiscal period?

7. How does the posting of the third closing entry affect the owner's equity?
8. How does the posting of the fourth closing entry affect the owner's equity?
9. Why are balance sheet accounts the only accounts listed on a post-closing trial balance?
10. What does the post-closing trial balance prove?

PROBLEMS

20–1 Refer to Problem 18–1. Using a four-column general journal, page 7, complete the following:

1) The adjusting entries.
2) The closing entries.

(1) and (2)   **GENERAL JOURNAL**   Page

Acct. Pay. Dr.	General Dr.	Date		PR	General Cr.	Acct. Rec. Cr.

20–2 Refer to Problem 18–2. Using a two-column general journal, page 6, do the following:
1) Record the adjusting entries and post.
2) Record the closing entries and post.
3) Take a post-closing trial balance.

(1) and (2)   **GENERAL JOURNAL**   Page

Date		Account Title	PR	Debit	Credit

(3)

20–3 Refer to Problem 19–3. Using a four-column general journal, page 9, do the following:
1) Record the adjusting entries.
2) Record the closing entries.

1) and (2)   GENERAL JOURNAL   Page

Acct. Pay. Dr.	General Cr.	Date		PR	General Dr.	Acct. Rec. Cr.

CYCLE TWO
EXAMINATION

Part I Indicate by a check (√) in the column at the right whether each statement is TRUE or FALSE.

	T	F
Example: Debts owed to creditors are accounts payable.	√	
1. A purchases journal is used for recording the purchase of all merchandise.		
2. Cost accounts increase by debits.		
3. A major advantage of special journals is the elimination of repetitive posting.		
4. A source document for each transaction is identified in the ledger account.		
5. A controlling account is found in each subsidiary ledger.		
6. A summary entry proves that debits equal credits in each journal.		
7. A check-mark posting reference to a customer's account indicates that the item has been posted.		
8. General Debit and General Credit column totals are posted to general ledger accounts.		
9. A subsidiary ledger's accuracy is proved by taking a trial balance.		
10. Invoices usually are prepared in multiple copies.		
11. The use of special journals eliminates the need for controlling accounts.		
12. A correcting entry usually is recorded in the general journal.		
13. A charge to the wrong customer's account is corrected by debiting that account and crediting the correct one.		
14. A withdrawal of merchandise by the owner is debited to the Sales account.		
15. A statement of account is sent to each charge customer to indicate the balance due.		
16. An eight-column work sheet includes special columns for closing entries.		
17. Prepaid expenses are adjusted at the end of each fiscal period by the amounts of their ending inventory values.		
18. Partners automatically share net income equally unless a written agreement specifies otherwise.		
19. Gross profit on sales is found by subtracting cost of goods sold from net sales.		
20. A post-closing trial balance includes general ledger accounts with adjusted balances.		

Part II Match the definition with the term by writing the appropriate *letter* in the column at the right. (A term is used once only.)

Terms		Definitions		Letter
	Example:	A charge purchase of merchandise, rather than a purchase for cash		K
A. Adjusting entries	1.	A special grouping of similar accounts	1.	
B. Capital statement	2.	A source document that describes a sale of merchandise	2.	
C. Cash disbursement	3.	The totaling of all special journals to prove that debits equal credits	3.	
D. Cash receipts journal	4.	A special journal for all cash payments	4.	
E. Closing entries credits	5.	The journal in which a withdrawal of merchandise by the owner is recorded.	5.	
F. Debit	6.	The normal balance of a customer's account	6.	
G. Credit	7.	A valuation account	7.	
H. General journal	8.	Entries made at the end of the fiscal period to bring certain accounts up to date	8.	
I. Income statement	9.	The financial statement that shows changes in owner's equity	9.	
J. Invoice	10.	Proving that general ledger debits and credits are equal	10.	
K. On account				
L. Purchases returns and allowances				
M. Subsidiary ledger				
N. Summary entry				
O. Trial balance				

Part III (1) Record each of the following transactions for Rex Drug Company in the journals provided:

June 1, Paid month's rent, $375; check No. 147

3, Purchased $500 worth of merchandise on account from J. L. Rossini Company

5, Sold merchandise on account to Dr. George Tyler, $165

8, The owner, Howard Craven, withdrew $50 worth of merchandise for personal use

10, Paid J. L. Rossini Company $500 on account; check No. 148

12, Issued credit memo No. 7 for $15 to Dr. George Tyler for merchandise returned

15, Cash sales to date were $2,950

19, Paid telephone bill, $46; check No. 149

22, Received $150 from Dr. George Tyler for balance due on account

26, Sold $125 worth of merchandise to Mel Guberman on account

29, Purchased $300 worth of merchandise from Fred Pulaski Wholesalers, Inc., on account

30, Cash sales to date were $3,750

(2) Summarize each journal, and checkmark any totals not to be posted.

1) and 2)   **GENERAL JOURNAL**   Page 3

Accts. Pay. Dr.	General Dr.	Date		PR	General Cr.	Accts. Rec. Cr.

1) and 2)   PURCHASES JOURNAL   Page 2

Date	Account Credited			PR	Purchases Dr. Accts. Pay. Cr.

1) and 2)   SALES JOURNAL   Page 4

Date	Account Debited		PR	Acct. Rec. Dr. Sales Cr.

1) and 2)   CASH RECEIPTS JOURNAL   Page 3

Date		PR	General Cr.	Accts. Rec. Cr.	Sales Cr.	Cash Dr.
198– June 1	Balance on hand $2,500	√				

(1) and (2)

CASH DISBURSEMENTS JOURNAL

Date	Account Debited	Ck. No.	PR	General Dr.	Accts. Pay. Dr.	Purchases Dr.	Salary Exp. Dr.	Cash Cr.

Part IV   From the completed work sheet below do the following:
  (1)   Prepare an income statement.
  (2)   Complete a capital statement, assuming that Fowler made a $1,000 investment during the fiscal period.
  (3)   Prepare a balance sheet.
  (4)   Journalize the adjusting and closing entries.

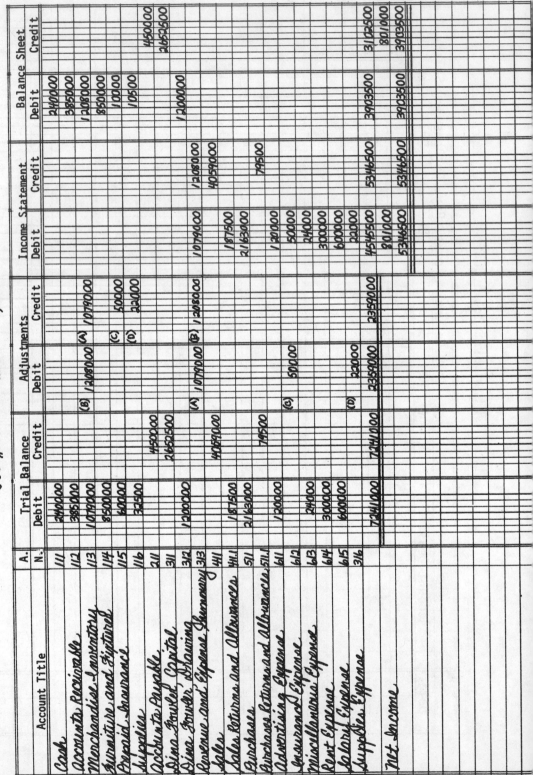

Fowler's Crystal Palace
Work Sheet
For Year Ended December 31, 198—

Account Title	A. N.	Trial Balance Debit	Trial Balance Credit	Adjustments Debit	Adjustments Credit	Income Statement Debit	Income Statement Credit	Balance Sheet Debit	Balance Sheet Credit
Cash	111	240000						240000	
Accounts Receivable	112	385000						385000	
Merchandise Inventory	113	1079000		(B) 1208000	(A) 1079000			1208000	
Furniture and Fixtures	114	850000						850000	
Prepaid Insurance	115	60000			(C) 50000			10000	
Supplies	116	32500			(D) 22000			10500	
Accounts Payable	211		450000						450000
Dina Fowler, Capital	311		2652500						2652500
Dina Fowler, Drawing	312	1200000						1200000	
Revenue and Expense Summary	313			(A) 1079000	(B) 1208000	1079000	1208000		
Sales	411		4059000				4059000		
Sales Returns and Allowances	411.1	187500				187500			
Purchases	511	2163000				2163000			
Purchases Returns and Allowances	511.1		79500				79500		
Advertising Expense	611	120000				120000			
Insurance Expense	612			(C) 50000		50000			
Miscellaneous Expense	613	240000				240000			
Rent Expense	614	300000				300000			
Salary Expense	615	600000				600000			
Supplies Expense	616			(D) 22000		22000			
		7241000	7241000	2359000	2359000	4545500	5346500	3903500	3102500
Net Income						801000			801000
						5346500	5346500	3903500	3903500

(1) _____

(2) _____

(3)

(4)

GENERAL JOURNAL   Page

Accts. Pay Dr.	General Dr.	Date		PR	General Cr.	Accts. Rec. Cr.

GENERAL JOURNAL   Page

Accts. Pay Dr.	General Dr.	Date		PR	General Cr.	Accts. Rec. Cr.

ANSWERS TO SELECTED QUESTIONS AND PROBLEMS

Chapter 2

QUESTIONS

	Classification	Side
1.	Asset	Left
2.	Liability	Right
3.	Owner's equity	Right
4.	Asset	Left
5.	Liability	Right
6.	Asset	Left
7.	Asset	Left
8.	Liability	Right
9.	Asset	Left
10.	Owner's equity	Right

PROBLEMS

2–1		A	=	L	+	OE
1.	Decrease		Decrease		
2.	None				
3.	Increase		Increase		
4.	None				
5.	None				
6.	Increase				Increase
7.	None				
8.	Decrease				Decrease

2-2	A	=	L	+	OE
1.	- $ 2,000				
	+ 2,000				
	$29,250		$ 4,250		$25,000
2.	+ 7,500		+ 7,500		
	$36,750		$11,750		$25,000
3.	- $ 450				
	+ 450				
	$36,750		$11,750		$25,000
4.	- $12,000				
	+ 12,000				
	$36,750		$11,750		$25,000
5.	- 1,500		- 1,500		
	$35,250		$10,250		$25,000

Chapter 3

3-1 Classification

1. Asset
2. Liability
3. Asset
4. Owner's equity
5. Asset
6. Asset
7. Liability
8. Liability
9. Owner's equity
10. Liability

3-2

	Right Side	Left Side
1.	Asset	
2.		Liability
3.	Asset	
4.		Liability
5.	Asset	
6.	Asset	
7.	Asset	
8.		Owner's equity
9.	Asset	
10.		Owner's equity

3-3 Total Assets, $11,250

Total Liabilities,	$ 2,7
Capital	8,4
Total Liab. + OE	$11,2

3-4 Total Assets, $7,685

Total Liabilities,	$ 8
Capital	6,8
Total Liab. + OE	$7,68

3-5 Total Assets, $1,389.50

Total Liabilities,	$ 197.
Capital	1,191.
Total Liab. + OE	$1,389.

3-6 Total Assets, $104,050

Total Liabilities,	$ 28,925.
Capital	75,125.
Total Liab. + OE	$104,050.

Chapter 4

4–1 (2)   Total Assets, $5,345

Total Liabilities,	$ 575
Capital	4,770
Total Liab. + OE	$5,345

Therefore:

Emilee Suzanne, Capital

	4770

4–2 (2)   Total Assets, $7,910

Total Liabilities,	$2,050
Capital	5,860
Total Liab. + OE	$7,910

4–5 (3)   Total Assets, $3,682.50

Total Liabilities,	$ 215.00
Capital	3,467.50
Total Liab. + OE	$3,682.50

Chapter 5

5–1

Cash	377.00
Taxis	28000.00
Supplies	150.00
Salary Expense	200.00
Gas and Oil Expense	45.00
Puccio, Drawing	300.00
Repair Expense	40.00
Total	29112.00
Landia	6300.00
Puccio, Capital	22237.00
Fare Income	575.00
Total	29112.00

5–2 (1)

Cash	902.00
Accounts Receivable	425.00
Delivery Equipment	12000.00
Supplies	160.00
Tucker, Drawing	600.00
Advertising Expense	95.00
Telephone Expense	140.00
Trucking Expense	150.00
Total	14472.00
Accounts Payable	1075.00
Tucker, Capital	12297.00
Delivery Income	1100.00
Total	14472.00

5–2 (2)   Total Assets, $13,487

Total Liabilities,	$ 1,075
Capital	12,412
Total Liab. + OE	$13,487

Chapter 6

6–1

| | | | | | JOURNAL | | | | Page 7 |

JOURNAL — Page 7

Date		Account Title	PR	Debit	Credit
198– Oct.	2	Salary Expense		17500	
		Cash			17500
		Employee's Salary			
	7	Cash		60000	
		Design Income			60000
		Received for a design			
	14	Supplies		20000	
		Cash			20000
		Supplies and material			
	16	Cash		100000	
		Vernon Trust Co.			100000
		Borrowed from bank			
	21	Cash		50000	
		Design Income			50000
		Received for a design			
	23	Equipment		36000	
		Cash			16000
		Textile Equipment Co.			20000
		new drawing table			
	30	Rose Klein, Drawing		40000	
		Cash			40000
		Withdrawal			
	31	Cash		10000	
		Mary Wu			10000
		Received on account			

Chapter 7

7–1 (ledger postings only)

Cash · No. 11

198–Oct.					198–Oct.				
Oct.	1	Balance	✓	1750 00	Oct.	18		6	500 00
	10		6	2500 00		25		6	250 00

Equipment · No. 12

198–Oct.				
Oct.	1	Balance	✓	3000 00
	1		6	1000 00

Landers Mfg. Company · No. 21

198–Oct.					198–Oct.				
Oct.	25		6	250 00	Oct.	1		6	1000 00

L. D. Berger, Drawing · No. 32

198–Oct.				
Oct.	18		6	500 00

Service Income · No. 41

				198–Oct.				
				Oct.	10		6	2500 00

7–2				7–3		
	Cash	2020.00			Cash	1275.00
	Equipment	3965.00			Equipment	1642.50
	Supplies	60.00			Supplies	355.00
	Kriss, Drawing	500.00			Schaffer, Drawing	300.00
	Advertising Expense	100.00			Miscellaneous Expense	65.00
	Utilities Expense	50.00			Total	3637.50
	Total	6695.00				
	Hi-Tech	1925.00			Jessup Bank	825.00
	Comp-Software	465.00			Schaffer, Capital	2372.50
	Kriss, Capital	3060.00			Fee Income	440.00
	Services Income	1245.00			Total	3637.50
	Total	6695.00				

Chapter 8

8–1

8–2 (2) Net Income, $1,450
8–3 (1) Trial Balance total, $11,777.50
8–3 (2) Net Income, $1,150.50

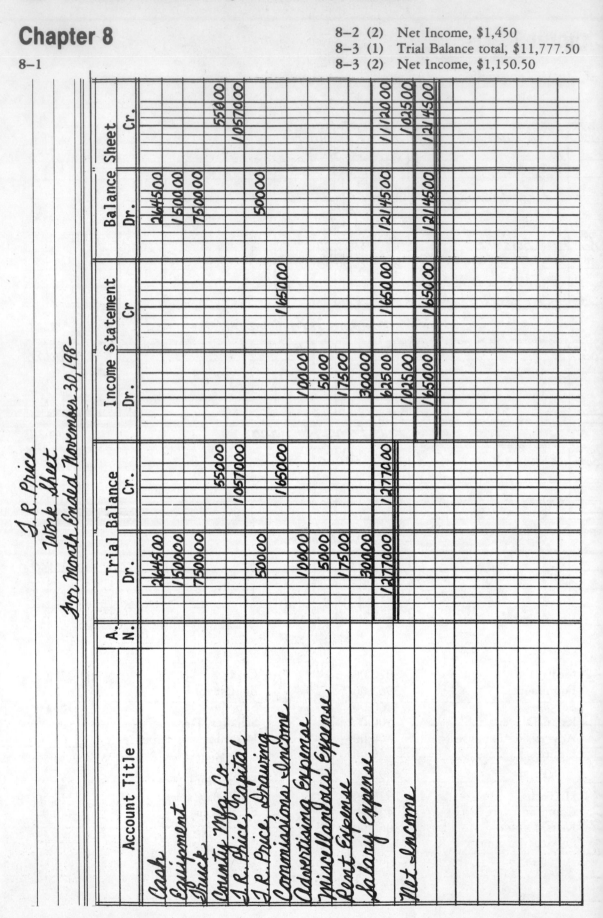

J.R. Price
Work Sheet
For month Ended November 30, 198-

Account Title	A. N.	Trial Balance Dr.	Trial Balance Cr.	Income Statement Dr.	Income Statement Cr	Balance Sheet Dr.	Balance Sheet Cr.
Cash		2645 00				2645 00	
Equipment		1500 00				1500 00	
Truck		7500 00				7500 00	
County Mfg. Co.			550 00				550 00
J.R. Price, Capital			1057000				1057000
J.R. Price, Drawing		500 00				500 00	
Commissions Income			165000		165000		
Advertising Expense		100 00		100 00			
Miscellaneous Expense		50 00		50 00			
Rent Expense		175 00		175 00			
Salary Expense		300 00		300 00			
		1277000	1277000	625 00	165000	1214500	1112000
Net Income				1025 00			1025 00
				165000	165000	1214500	1214500

Chapter 9

9–1 (a)

J. R. Price
Income Statement
For Month Ended November 30, 198–

Revenue:		
Commissions Income		1650 00
Expenses:		
Advertising Expense	100 00	
Miscellaneous Expense	50 00	
Rent Expense	175 00	
Salary Expense	300 00	
Total Expenses		625 00
Net Income		1025 00

9–1 (b)

J. R. Price
Capital Statement
For Month Ended November 30, 198–

Beginning Balance, Nov. 1, 198–		10570 00
Plus: Net Income	1025 00	
Less: Withdrawals	500 00	
Net Increase in Capital		525 00
Ending Balance, Nov. 30, 198–		11095 00

9–1 (c)

J. R. Price
Balance Sheet
November 30, 198–

Assets		Liabilities	
Cash	2645 00	County Mfg. Company	550 00
Equipment	1500 00	Owners' Equity	
Truck	7500 00	J. R. Price, Capital, Nov. 30	11095 00
Total Assets	11645 00	Total Liab. & O.E.	11645 00

9–3 (b) Capital, October 31, 198–, $6,852.50

9–4 (1) Trial Balance totals:

5648.00	8600.00
10400.00	28243.00
420.00	3680.00
2655.00	40523.00
15000.00	
400.00	
1500.00	
2500.00	
800.00	
1200.00	
40523.00	

Net Loss, $220

9–4 (2)(b) Decrease in Capital, $2,720
Capital, November 30, 198–
$25,523

Chapter 10

10–1 Net Income, $3,350 from completed Income Statement columns on work sheet

			Closing Entries			
198– Dec.	31		Consulting Fees Income	3750 00		
			Royalty Income	500 00		
			Revenue and Expense, Summary			4250 00
	31		Revenue and Expense, Summary	900 00		
			Advertising Expense			100 00
			Miscellaneous Expense			60 00
			Rent Expense			250 00
			Salary Expense			400 00
			Telephone Expense			90 00
	31		Revenue and Expense, Summary	3350 00		
			Gwen Vreeland, Capital			3350 00
	31		Gwen Vreeland, Capital	1800 00		
			Gwen Vreeland, Drawing			1800 00

10–2 Trial Balance amounts:

800.00	6000.00
3895.00	12920.00
4000.00	6500.00
12500.00	Total 25420.00
750.00	
1500.00	
600.00	
175.00	
300.00	
900.00	
Total 25420.00	

Net Income, $4525.00

10–3 (1)   Trial Balance totals, $35,675.75
           Net Income, $4,850.00 (on completed
           work sheet)

10–3 (2)(b)

Earl Alpert
Capital Statement
June 30, 198–

Beginning Balance, April 1		2330075
Plus: Additional Investment	100000	
Net Income	485000	
	585000	
Less: Withdrawals	480000	
Net Increase in Capital		105000
Ending Balance, June 30, 198–		2435075

Chapter 11

11–1

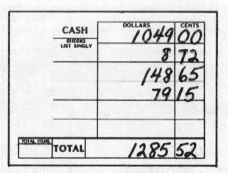

CASH	DOLLARS	CENTS
CHECKS LIST SINGLY	1049	00
	8	72
	148	65
	79	15
TOTAL	1285	52

11–2   Balance carried forward on stub No. 120,
      $106.50

11–3   Correct available balance, $416.90

11–4   Correct available balance, $705.32

Chapter 12

12-1 (3) Replenishing check drawn for $32.25

12-2

198-apr.	1	Petty Cash		3500	
		Cash			3500
		To establish fund			
	30	Auto Expense		1000	
		Delivery Expense		275	
		Miscellaneous Expense		750	
		Office Expense		1200	
		Cash			3225
		To replenish fund			

Cycle One Examination

Part I

1.	T	11.	T
2.	F	12.	T
3.	T	13.	F
4.	T	14.	T
5.	F	15.	F
6.	T	16.	T
7.	T	17.	T
8.	F	18.	F
9.	F	19.	F
10.	F	20.	T

Part II

1.	I	9.	V
2.	L	10.	E
3.	Q	11.	B
4.	U	12.	N
5.	F	13.	A
6.	G	14.	K
7.	R	15.	H
8.	T		

Part III

	Account Dr.	Account Cr.
1.	J	A
2.	B	A
3.	A	D
4.	G	F
5.	B	A, C
6.	E	A
7.	F	H, I, J
8.	F	D
9.	D	F
10.	D	E

Part IV (1)   Net Income, $10,820. Work sheet
Trial Balance totals, $34,275.00

Part IV (2)

County-Wide Plumbing
Capital Statement
December 31, 198—

Beginning Capital, Jan. 1, 198—		9685 00
Plus: Additional Investment	5000 00	
Net Income	10820 00	
	15820 00	
Less: Withdrawals	9500 00	
Net Increase in Capital		6320 00
Ending Capital, Dec. 31, 198—		16005 00

Part IV (3)

County-Wide Plumbing
Balance Sheet
December 31, 198—

Assets		Liabilities	
Cash	14772 50	Accounts Payable	970 00
Petty Cash	25 00	Owners' Equity	
Accounts Receivable	385 00	Chet Gorski, Capital	16005 00
Supplies	242 50		
Truck	1485 00	Total Liabilities +	
Total Assets	16975 00	Owners' Equity	16975 00

Part IV (4)

GENERAL JOURNAL

			Closing Entries		
198- Dec.	31	Fees Income		1862000	
			Revenue and Expense Summary		1862000
	31	Revenue and Expense Summary		780000	
			Advertising Expense		48000
			Automobile Expense		240000
			Miscellaneous Expense		12000
			Rent Expense		360000
			Telephone Expense		120000
	31	Revenue and Expense Summary		1082000	
			Chet Gorski, Capital		1082000
	31	Chet Gorski, Capital		950000	
			Chet Gorski, Drawing		950000

Part V (1)

	DOLLARS	CENTS
NO. 207 $35.50		
DATE January 7 198-		
TO Wilson Supply Co.		
FOR Smoke Alarm		
(Equipment)		
BAL. BRO'T FOR'D	382	47
AMT. DEPOSITED	225	00
TOTAL	607	47
AMT. THIS CHECK	35	50
BAL. CAR'D FOR'D	571	97

No. 207

1-830
860

January 7 198-

Pay to the order of   Wilson Supply Company $35 50

Thirty-five & 50/100 ———————— Dollars

BOLTON NATIONAL BANK
of New York, NY

Student's Name

⑆0860⑈0830⑆ 1248⑈671⑆

Part V (2)

JOURNAL

198– Jan.	7	Equipment				3550	
		Cash					3550
		Bought smoke alarm					

Chapter 13

13–1 (1) and (3)

PURCHASES JOURNAL — Page 5

Date		From Whom Purchased Account Credited		Invoice No.	PR	Purchases Dr. Acct. Pay. Cr.
198– Feb.	3	Dye + Akins		1705	✓	300 00
	10	Edward Kalpakian + Sons		G-116	✓	425 00
	17	Dye + Akins		1751	✓	385 00
	25	Edward Kalpakian + Sons		G-151	✓	500 00
	28	Total				1610 00
						(51) (21)

13–1 (2)

ACCOUNTS PAYABLE LEDGER

Dye & Akins
1011 Mountain Avenue, Denver, CO 80201

			PR	Dr.	Cr.	Cr. Bal.
198– Feb.	3		P5		300 00	300 00
	17		P5		385 00	685 00

Edward Kalpakian & Sons
379 Valley View Drive, Denver, CO 80204

			PR	Dr.	Cr.	Cr. Bal.
198– Feb.	10		P5		425 00	425 00
	25		P5		500 00	925 00

13–1 (3)

GENERAL LEDGER

Accounts Payable   No.

			PR	Dr.	Cr.	Balance Dr.	Balance Cr.
198– Feb.	28		P5		1610 00		1610

Purchases   No.

			PR	Dr.	Cr.	Balance Dr.	Balance Cr.
198– Feb.	28		P5	1610 00		1610 00	

1 (4)

Ruth Ann Davis
Schedule of Accounts Payable
February 28, 198—

Dye & Akins		685 00
Edward Kalpakian & Sons		925 00
Total Accounts Payable		1 610 00

2 (4)

Paul Zagretti
Schedule of Accounts Payable
February 28, 198—

Glen Mfg., Inc.		620 00
Island Supply		565 00
Paul Olino		535 00
Gregory Sims		250 00
Wilson & Shea		600 00
Total Accounts Payable		2 570 00

Chapter 14

14–1 (1) and (2)

CASH DISBURSEMENTS JOURNAL Page 3

Date	Account Debited	Ck. No.	PR	General Dr.	Acct. Pay. Dr.	S. Krasnoff Draw. Dr.	Cash Cr.
198– mar. 1	Rent Expense	247		400 00			400 00
3	Utilities Expense	248		76 50			76 50
8	Paula Cory	249			50 00		50 00
10	Sid Krasnoff, Drawing	250	✓			500 00	500 00
17	Salary Expense	251		300 00			300 00
22	Hilda Piper	252			90 00		90 00
24	Sid Krasnoff, Drawing	253				500 00	500 00
29	Equipment	254		1 250 00			1 250 00
31	Salary Expense	255		300 00			300 00
31	Totals			2 326 50	140 00	1 000 00	3 466 50
				(✓)	( )	( )	( )

14–2 (1), (2), and (4)

PURCHASES JOURNAL Page

Date	Account Credited	Invoice No.	PR	Purchases Dr. Acct. Pay. Cr.
198– apr. 4	Abel Jenks	P-311	✓	600 00
20	W. J. Gross	5-113	✓	1 450 00
30	Total			2 050 00
				2 050 00
				(51) (21)

14–2 (1), (3), and (4)

CASH DISBURSEMENTS JOURNAL Page 3

Date	Acct. Dr.	Ck. No.	PR	General Dr.	Acct. Pay. Dr.	Cash Cr.
198– apr. 1	Rent Expense	502	65	45000		45000
8	Helen Scordas, Drawing	503	32	40000		40000
14	Abel & Jenks	504	✓		80000	80000
15	Salary Expense	505	67	32500		32500
22	Supplies	506	15	7500		7500
28	Helen Scordas, Drawing	507	32	50000		50000
30	W. J. Gross	508	✓		72500	72500
30	Totals			175000	152500	327500
				(✓)	(21)	( )

14–2 (2) and (3)

ACCOUNTS PAYABLE LEDGER

Abel & Jenks
140 Rocky Mountain Street, Boise, ID 83101

Date		PR	Dr.	Cr.	Cr. Bal.
198– Apr. 1	Balance	✓			80000
4		P2		60000	140000
14		CD3	80000		60000

W. J. Gross
205 Columbia Avenue, Boise, ID 83702

Date		PR	Dr.	Cr.	Cr. Bal.
198– apr. 20		P2		145000	145000
30		CD3	72500		72500

Cash   No. 11

Date		PR	Dr.	Cr.	Balance Dr.	Cr.
198– apr. 1	Balance	✓			450000	
30		CD3		327500	122500	

(continued)

14–2 (2) and (3)

Supplies   No. 15

Date		PR	Dr.	Cr.	Balance Dr.	Cr.
198– apr. 1	Balance	✓			5000	
22		CD3	7500		12500	

Accounts Payable   No 21

Date		PR	Dr.	Cr.	Balance Dr.	Cr.
198– apr. 1	Balance	✓				80000
30		P2		205000		285000
30		CD3	152500			132500

Helen Scordas, Drawing   No. 32

Date		PR	Dr.	Cr.	Balance Dr.	Cr.
198– apr. 8		CD3	40000		40000	
28		CD3	50000		90000	

Purchases   No. 51

Date		PR	Dr.	Cr.	Balance Dr.	Cr.
198– apr. 30		P2	205000		205000	

Rent Expense   No. 65

Date		PR	Dr.	Cr.	Balance Dr.	Cr.
198– apr. 1		CD3	45000		45000	

Salary Expense   No. 67

Date		PR	Dr.	Cr.	Balance Dr.	Cr.
198– apr. 15		CD3	32500		32500	

14–2 (5)

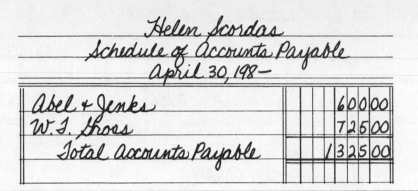

Helen Scordas Schedule of Accounts Payable April 30, 198–		
Abel & Jenks		600 00
W. I. Gross		725 00
Total Accounts Payable		1325 00

Chapter 15

15–1 (1), (2), and (3)

SALES JOURNAL   Page 31

Date	To Whom Sold – Account Debited	Invoice No.	PR	Acct. Rec. Dr Sales Cr.
198– Mar. 2	Mrs. Edward Ardyce	215	✓	175 00
9	Mr. Herman Gold	216	✓	96 50
16	Ms. Eliza Fisher	217	✓	107 30
23	Mrs. Edward Ardyce	218	✓	62 45
30	Ms. Eliza Fisher	219	✓	29 50
31	Total			470 75
				(13) (41)

15–1 (2)

ACCOUNTS RECEIVABLE LEDGER

Mrs. Edward Ardyce
305 Riverview Terrace, Cincinnati, OH 45204

Date				Dr.	Cr.	Dr. Bal.
198– Mar. 2		S31		175 00		175 00
23		S31		62 45		237 45

Ms. Eliza Fisher
851 Clarkfield Street, Cincinnati, OH 45201

Date				Dr.	Cr.	Dr. Bal.
198– Mar. 16		S31		107 30		107 30
30		S31		29 50		136 80

(continued)

15–1 (2)

Mr. Herman Gold
79 Willowbrook Drive, Cincinnati, OH 45202

			Dr.	Cr.	Dr. Bal.
198–mar.	1	Balance	✓		258 60
	9		S31	96 50	355 10

GENERAL LEDGER

15–1 (3)

Accounts Receivable

No. 13

			Dr.	Cr.	Balance Dr.	Balance Cr.
198–mar.	1	Balance	✓			258 60	
	31		S31	470 75		729 35	

Sales

No. 4

			Dr.	Cr.	Balance Dr.	Balance Cr.
198–mar.	31		S31		470 75		470 75

15–1 (4)

Mears Department Store
Schedule of Accounts Receivable
March 31, 198–

Mrs. Edward Ardyce	237 45
Ms. Eliza Fisher	136 80
Mr. Herman Gold	355 10
Total Accounts Receivable	729 35

15–2 (4)

Winslow's Emporium
Schedule of Accounts Receivable
April 30, 198–

Ms. Shirley Callahan	276 60
Mrs. Marjorie Intrator	144 55
Mrs. Fay Wilamowski	165 70
Mr. William Witt	203 45
Total Accounts Receivable	790 30

Chapter 16

16–1 (1), (2), and (3)

CASH RECEIPTS JOURNAL   Page 6

Date	Account Credited	PR	General Cr.	Accts. Rec. Cr.	Sales Cr.	Cash Dr.
198– Apr. 23		✓	750 00	1435 00	5976 00	8161 00
23	Raul Garcia, Capital		2000 00			2000 00
24	Lone Star Bank		2500 00			2500 00
25	J. R. Dallas			85 00		85 00
26	Margo Chase			60 00		60 00
27	Equipment		95 00			95 00
28	Frances Lima			75 00		75 00
29	Sales	✓			1765 00	1765 00
30	Totals		5345 00	1655 00	7741 00	14741 00
			(✓)	(13)	(41)	(11)

(Note: In a complete problem, items listed in the
General Cr. and Accts. Rec. Cr. columns
would be posted. Post references
would appear, therefore, in the PR column.)

16—1 (3)

GENERAL LEDGER

Cash
No. 11

Date			PR	Dr.	Cr.	Balance Dr.	Balance Cr.
198- Apr.	1	Balance	✓			1935 00	
	30		CR6	1474 00		1667 00	

Accounts Receivable
No. 13

Date			PR	Dr.	Cr.	Balance Dr.	Balance Cr.
198- Apr.	1	Balance	✓			1828 90	
	30		CR6		1655 00	73 50	

Sales
No. 41

Date			PR	Dr.	Cr.	Balance Dr.	Balance Cr.
198- Mar.	31		S4		3500 00		3500 00
	31		CR5		6250 00		9750 00
	31		J3	9750 00			—
Apr.	30		CR6		7741 00		7741 00

16—2 (1) and (2)

SALES JOURNAL
Page

Date		To Whom Sold - Account Debited	Invoice No.	PR	Acct. Rec. Dr. Sales Cr.
198- May	1	Willow's Beauty Shoppe	7156	✓	465 00
	1	Lee's Unisex	7157	✓	395 00
	12	Goddess of Love	7158	✓	268 00
	12	Jayne's Curls + Waves	7159	✓	175 00
	17	Willow's Beauty Shoppe	7160	✓	192 00
	29	Jayne's Curls + Waves	7161	✓	225 00
	29	Lee's Unisex	7162	✓	315 20
	31	Total			2035 70
					(13) (41)

16–2 (1) and (2)

CASH RECEIPTS JOURNAL

Page 6

Date	Account Credited	PR	General Cr.	Accts. Rec. Cr.	Sales Cr.	Cash Dr.
198– May 7	Sales	✓			252 50	252 50
10	Goddess of Love	✓		200 00		200 00
14	Sales	✓			307 25	307 25
15	Pat Norrell, Capital	31	3000 00			3000 00
19	Lee's Unisex	✓		395 00		395 00
21	Sales	✓			296 80	296 80
25	Willow's Beauty Shoppe	✓		265 00		265 00
28	Sales	✓			319 90	319 90
31	Sales	✓			191 40	191 40
31	Totals		3000 00	860 00	1367 85	5227 85
			(✓)	(13)	(41)	(11)

16–2 (1) and (2)

GENERAL LEDGER

Cash

No. 11

Date		PR	Dr.	Cr.	Balance Dr.	Balance Cr.
198– May 1	Balance	✓			1078 50	
31		CR6	5227 85		6306 35	

Accounts Receivable

No. 13

Date			Dr.	Cr.	Balance Dr.	Balance Cr.
198– May 1	Balance	✓			200 00	
31		S9	2035 70		2235 70	
		CR6		860 00	1375 70	

Pat Norrell, Capital

No. 31

Date			Dr.	Cr.	Balance Dr.	Balance Cr.
198– May 1	Balance	✓				25000 00
15		CR6		3000 00		28000 00

Sales

No. 41

Date			Dr.	Cr.	Balance Dr.	Balance Cr.
198– May 31		S9		2035 70		2035 70
31		CR6		1367 85		3403 55

16–2 (1) and (2)

ACCOUNTS RECEIVABLE LEDGER

Goddess of Love
110 Chemung Avenue, Binghamton, NY 13901

Date		PR	Dr.	Cr.	Dr. Bal.
198– may 1	Balance	✓			200 00
10		CR6		200 00	—
12		S9	268 50		268 50

Jayne's Curls & Waves
39 Tompkins Avenue, Cortland, NY 13045

Date		PR	Dr.	Cr.	Dr. Bal.
198– may 12		S9	175 00		175 00
29		S9	225 00		400 00

16–2 (1) and (2)

Lee's Unisex
451 College Heights Road, Ithaca, NY 14850

Date		PR	Dr.	Cr.	Dr. Bal.
198– may 1		S9	395 00		395 00
19		CR6		395 00	—
29		S9	315 20		315 20

Willow's Beauty Shoppe
58 Swain Boulevard, Elmira, NY 14901

Date		PR	Dr.	Cr.	Dr. Bal.
198– may 1		S9	465 00		465 00
17		S9	192 00		657 00
25		CR6		265 00	392 00

16–2 (4)

Pat Norvell
Schedule of Accounts Receivable
May 31, 198–

Goddess of Love	268 50
Jayne's Curls + Waves	400 00
Lee's Unisex	315 20
Willow's Beauty Shoppe	392 00
Total Accounts Receivable	1375 70

Chapter 17

7–1 (1) and (2)

GENERAL JOURNAL   Page 7

Accts. Pay. Dr.	General Dr.	Date		PR	General Cr.	Accts. Rec. Cr.
	35 00	198– May 2	Sales Returns + Allowances			
			Jane McDonald			35 00
			Credit Memo No. 18			
	65 00	5	Hedy Nachtigal		65 00	
			Netty Nachtigal			
			Correct posting error			
100 00		9	Baldwin Piano Company			
			Purchases Returns + Allowances		100 00	
			Debit Memo No. 53			
	95 00	15	Philip Scheiber, Drawing			
			Purchases		95 00	
			Withdrew guitar for nephew			
	80 00	22	Sales Returns + Allowances			
			Alice Glaser			80 00
			Credit Memo No. 19			
	185 00	29	Equipment			
			Philip Scheiber, Capital		185 00	
			Invested desk			
100 00	460 00	31	Totals		445 00	115 00
	(✓)				(✓)	

17–3

STATEMENT OF ACCOUNT

Hudson's Department Store
100 Gateway Plaza
St. Louis, MO 63101

SOLD TO

May 20　19 8–

Ms. Pearl Nathanson
972 Riverside Dr.
St. Louis, MO 63104

		CHARGES							
May	1		60	00					
	5		75	00					
	18		45	00					
						180	00		
		PAYMENTS/CREDITS							
	12		35	00					
	15		20	00					
						55	00		
	18	Balance Due				125	00		

17–4 (1) and (2)

PURCHASES JOURNAL

Page 10

Date		Account Credited			PR	Purchases Dr. Acct. Pay. Cr.
198– May	17	Schmidt + Brendle				375 00
	17	Winston Jewelers				1200 00
	31	Totals				1575 00
						( ) ( )

17–4 (1) and (2)

SALES JOURNAL

Page 14

Date		Account Debited	Invoice No.	PR	Accts. Rec. Dr. Sales Cr.
198– May	4	Antonio Lorenzo	B192		300 00
	4	Edward Grabozak	B193		250 00
	11	Marc Green	B194		275 00
	31	Totals			825 00
					( ) ( )

17–4 (1)

CASH RECEIPTS JOURNAL

Page 19

Date				PR	Gen. Cr.	Acct. Rec. Cr.	Sales Cr.	Cash Dr.
198– May	1	Balance on hand	$1,500	✓				
	3	Marc Green				150 00		150 00
	3	Gian Polidoro				95 00		95 00
	22	Antonio Lorenzo				50 00		50 00
	23	Edward Grabozak				125 00		125 00
	31	Sales		✓			2740 00	2740 00
	31	Totals			—	420 00	2740 00	3160 00
					(✓)	( )	( )	( )

17–4 (1)

CASH DISBURSEMENTS JOURNAL

Date		Ck. No.	PR	Gen. Dr.	Accts. Pay. Dr.	Purch. Dr.	Cash Cr.
198– may 1	Winslow Jewelers	392			46500		46500
1	Rent Expense	393		45000			45000
13	Edward Shaw, Drawing	394		50000			50000
14	Salary Expense	395		30000			30000
28	Schmidt & Brendle	396			37500		37500
29	Sales Returns & Allowances	397		4000			4000
31	Totals			129000	84000		213000
				(✓)	( )		( )

17–4 (1)

GENERAL JOURNAL   Page 5

Acct. Pay. Dr.	Gen. Dr.	Date		PR	Gen. Cr.	Acct. Rec. Cr.
	3500	198– may 8	Supplies			
			Equipment		3500	
			Posting Error			
7500		24	Sales Returns & Allowances			
			Marc Green			7500
			Credit Memo No. 35			
	20000	31	Edward Shaw, Drawing			
			Purchases		20000	
			Ring for wife			
	31000	31	Totals		23500	7500
(–)	(✓)				(✓)	( )

Chapter 18

18–1

Daniel Green
Work Sheet
For Quarter Year Ended June 30, 19—

Account Title	A.N.	Trial Balance Debit	Trial Balance Credit	Adjustments Debit	Adjustments Credit	Income Statement Debit	Income Statement Credit	Balance Sheet Debit	Balance Sheet Credit
Cash		120000						120000	
Accounts Receivable		350000						350000	
Merchandise Inventory		500000		(B) 517500	(A) 500000			517500	
Equipment		600000						600000	
Supplies		40000			(C) 10000			30000	
Accounts Payable			180000						180000
Daniel Green, Capital			1420000						1420000
Daniel Green, Drawing		150000						150000	
Revenue and Expense Summary				(A) 500000	(B) 517500	500000	517500		
Sales			650000				650000		
Sales Returns & Allowances		25000				25000			
Purchases		300000				300000			
Purchases Returns & Allowances			15000				15000		
Miscellaneous Expense		10000				10000			
Rent Expense		120000				120000			
Salary Expense		150000				150000			
Supplies Expense				(C) 10000		10000			
		2365000	2365000	1027500	1027500	1115000	1182500	1675000	1600000
Net Income						67500			67500
						1182500	1182500	1667500	1667500

18–2

Timothy Sullivan
Work Sheet
For Month Ended January 31, 19—

Account Title	A.N.	Trial Balance Debit	Trial Balance Credit	Adjustments Debit	Adjustments Credit	Income Statement Debit	Income Statement Credit	Balance Sheet Debit	Balance Sheet Credit
Cash		336000						336000	
Accounts Receivable		351500						351500	
Merchandise Inventory		380000		(B) 395000	(A) 380000			395000	
Supplies		32500			(C) 12000			20500	
Prepaid Insurance		30000			(D) 5000			25000	
Accounts Payable			180000						180000
Timothy Sullivan, Capital			787500						787500
Timothy Sullivan, Drawing		30000						30000	
Expense and Expense Summary				(A) 380000	(B) 395000	380000	395000		
Sales			420000				420000		
Sales Returns and Allowances		3500				3500			
Purchases		170000				170000			
Advertising Expense		10000				10000			
Insurance Expense				(D) 5000		5000			
Miscellaneous Expense		4000				4000			
Rent Expense		40000				40000			
Supplies Expense				(C) 12000		12000			
		1387500	1387500	792000	792000	624500	815000	1158000	967500
Net Income						190500			190500
						815000	815000	1158000	1158000

Chapter 19

19–1 (1)

<table>
<tr><td colspan="3" align="center">Daniel Green</td></tr>
<tr><td colspan="3" align="center">Income Statement</td></tr>
<tr><td colspan="3" align="center">For Quarter Ended April 30, 198—</td></tr>
<tr><td>Income:</td><td></td><td></td></tr>
<tr><td>Sales</td><td>6500 00</td><td></td></tr>
<tr><td>Less Sales Returns and Allowances</td><td>250 00</td><td></td></tr>
<tr><td>Net Sales</td><td></td><td>6250 00</td></tr>
<tr><td>Cost of Goods Sold:</td><td></td><td></td></tr>
<tr><td>Merchandise Inventory, Apr. 1</td><td>5000 00</td><td></td></tr>
<tr><td>Purchases   3000</td><td></td><td></td></tr>
<tr><td>Less Purchases Ret. + Allow   150</td><td></td><td></td></tr>
<tr><td>Net Purchases</td><td>2850 00</td><td></td></tr>
<tr><td>Merchandise Available for Sale</td><td>7850 00</td><td></td></tr>
<tr><td>Less Merchandise Inv., June 30</td><td>5175 00</td><td></td></tr>
<tr><td>Cost of Goods Sold</td><td></td><td>2675 00</td></tr>
<tr><td>Gross Profit on Sales</td><td></td><td>3575 00</td></tr>
<tr><td>Expenses:</td><td></td><td></td></tr>
<tr><td>Miscellaneous Expense</td><td>100 00</td><td></td></tr>
<tr><td>Rent Expense</td><td>1200 00</td><td></td></tr>
<tr><td>Salary Expense</td><td>1500 00</td><td></td></tr>
<tr><td>Supplies Expense</td><td>100 00</td><td></td></tr>
<tr><td>Total Expense</td><td></td><td>2900 00</td></tr>
<tr><td>Net Income</td><td></td><td>675 00</td></tr>
</table>

19–1 (2)

Daniel Green

Capital Statement

For Quarter Ended June 30, 198–

Beginning Balance, April 1		12200 00
Additional Investment		2000 00
		14200 00
Less: Withdrawals	1500 00	
Less Net Income	675 00	
Net Decrease in Capital		825 00
Ending Balance, June 30		13375 00

19–1 (3)

Daniel Green

Balance Sheet

June 30, 198–

Assets		
Cash	1200 00	
Accounts Receivable	2500 00	
Merchandise Inventory	5175 00	
Equipment	6000 00	
Supplies	300 00	
Total Assets		15175 00
Liabilities		
Accounts Payable		1800 00
Owner's Equity		13375 00
Total Liabilities and Owner's Equity		15175 00

9–2 (2)

Timothy Sullivan Capital Statement For Month Ended January 31, 198–			
Beginning Balance, Jan. 1			5375 00
Additional Investment			2500 00
			7875 00
Plus: Net Income	1905 00		
Less Withdrawals	300 00		
Net Increase in Capital			1605 00
Ending Balance, Jan. 31			9480 00

9–2 (3)   Assets $11,280 = Liabilities $1,800
+ Owner's Equity $9,480.

19–3 (1)

Abdullah and Pahlavi
Work Sheet
For Year Ended December 31, 198—

Account Title	A.N.	Trial Balance Debit	Trial Balance Credit	Adjustments Debit	Adjustments Credit	Income Statement Debit	Income Statement Credit	Balance Sheet Debit	Balance Sheet Credit
Cash		3615.00						3615.00	
Accounts Receivable		18260.00						18260.00	
Merchandise Inventory, Jan. 1		22320.00		(B) 23195.00	(A) 22320.00			23195.00	
Equipment		7500.00						7500.00	
Prepaid Insurance		500.00			(C) 100.00			400.00	
Supplies		275.00			(D) 96.50			178.50	
Accounts Payable			3105.00						3105.00
J.H. Abdullah, Capital			33802.00						33802.00
J.H. Abdullah, Drawing		10000.00						10000.00	
J.H. Pahlavi, Capital			28404.00						28404.00
J.H. Pahlavi, Drawing		12000.00						12000.00	
Revenue and Expense Summary				(A) 22320.00	(B) 23195.00	22320.00	23195.00		
Sales			51790.00				51790.00		
Sales Returns and Allowances		2570.00				2570.00			
Purchases		31380.00				31380.00			
Purchases Returns and Allowances			1529.00				1529.00		
Advertising Expense		600.00				600.00			
Insurance Expense				(C) 100.00		100.00			
Rent Expense		3600.00				3600.00			
Salary Expense		6000.00				6000.00			
Supplies Expense				(D) 96.50		96.50			
		118630.00	118630.00	45711.50	45711.50	66666.50	76514.00	75158.50	65311.00
Net Income						9847.50			9847.50
						76514.00	76514.00	75158.50	75158.50

Chapter 20

20–1 (1) and (2)

GENERAL JOURNAL   Page 7

			Adjusting Entries	
5000 00	198– June	30	Revenue and Expense Summary	
			Merchandise Inventory	5000 00
5175 00		30	Merchandise Inventory	
			Revenue and Expense Summary	5175 00
100 00		30	Supplies Expense	
			Supplies	100 00
			Closing Entries	
6500 00		30	Sales	
150 00			Purchases Returns and Allowances	
			Revenue and Expense Summary	6650 00
6150 00		30	Revenue and Expense Summary	
			Sales Returns and Allowances	250 00
			Purchases	3000 00
			Miscellaneous Expense	100 00
			Rent Expense	1200 00
			Salary Expense	1500 00
			Supplies Expense	100 00
675 00		30	Revenue and Expense Summary	
			Daniel Green, Capital	675 00
1500 00		30	Daniel Green, Capital	
			Daniel Green, Drawing	1500 00

20–2 (3)

Timothy Sullivan
Post-closing Trial Balance
January 31, 198–

Cash	3360 00	
Accounts Receivable	3515 00	
Merchandise Inventory	3950 00	
Supplies	205 00	
Prepaid Insurance	250 00	
Accounts Payable		1800 00
Timothy Sullivan, Capital		9480 00
Totals	11280 00	11280 00

20–3 (3)

Abdullah and Pahlevi
Post-closing Trial Balance
December 31, 198–

Cash	3625 00	
Accounts Receivable	18260 00	
Merchandise Inventory	23195 00	
Equipment	7500 00	
Prepaid Insurance	400 00	
Supplies	178 50	
Accounts Payable		3105 00
J. H. Abdullah, Capital		29429 14
S. H. Pahlevi, Capital		20624 36
Totals	53158 50	53158 50

Cycle Two Examination

Part I

1.	T	11.	F
2.	T	12.	T
3.	T	13.	F
4.	F	14.	F
5.	F	15.	T
6.	T	16.	F
7.	T	17.	F
8.	F	18.	T
9.	F	19.	T
10.	T	20.	T

Part II

1.	M	6.	F
2.	J	7.	L
3.	N	8.	A
4.	C	9.	B
5.	H	10.	O

Part III (1)

GENERAL JOURNAL   Page 3

Accts. Pay. Dr.	General Dr.	Date		PR	General Cr.	Accts. Rec Cr.
	5000	98— June 8	Howard Craven, Drawing			
			Purchases		5000	
			Withdrew Merchandise			
1500		12	Sales Returns and Allowances			
			Dr. George Tyler			1500
6500		30	Totals		5000	1500
(✓)					(✓)	( )

Part III (1)

PURCHASES JOURNAL   Page 3

Date	Account Credited			PR	Purchases Dr. Accts. Pay. Cr.
98— June 3	J. L. Rossini Company				50000
29	Fred Pulaski Wholesalers, Inc.				30000
30	Total				80000
					( ) ( )

Part III (1)

SALES JOURNAL
Page 3

Date	Account Debited		PR	Accts. Rec. Dr. Sales Cr.
198- June 5	Dr. George Tyler			1650 00
26	Mel Guberman			1250 00
30	Total			2900 00
				( ) ( )

Part III (1)

CASH RECEIPTS JOURNAL
Page 4

Date		PR	General Cr.	Accts. Rec. Cr.	Sales Cr.	Cash Dr.
198- June 1	Balance on hand $2,500	✓				
15	Sales	✓			2950 00	2950 00
22	Dr. George Tyler			150 00		150 00
30	Sales	✓			3750 00	3750 00
30	Totals			150 00	6700 00	6850 00
			(✓)	( )	( )	( )

Part III (1)

CASH DISBURSEMENTS JOURNAL
Page 3

Date	Account Debited	Ck. No.	PR	General Dr.	Accts. Pay Dr.	Purchases Dr.	Salary Exp. Dr.	Cash Cr.
198- June 1	Rent Expense	147		375 00				375 00
10	J. L. Rossini Company	148			500 00			500 00
19	Telephone (Utilities) Expense	149		46 00				46 00
30	Totals			421 00	500 00			921 00
				(✓)	( )			( )

Part IV (1)

Fowler's Crystal Palace
Income Statement
For Year Ended December 31, 198–

Income:		
Sales	4059000	
Less, Sales Returns and Allowances	187500	
Net Sales		3871500
Cost of Goods Sold:		
Merchandise Inventory, Jan. 1	1079000	
Purchases 21,630		
Less Purchases Ret + Allow. 795		
Net Purchases	2083500	
Merchandise Available for Sale	3162500	
Less Merchandise Inventory, Dec. 3	1208000	
Cost of Goods Sold		1954500
Gross Profit on Sales		1917000
Expenses:		
Advertising Expense	120000	
Insurance Expense	50000	
Miscellaneous Expense	24000	
Rent Expense	300000	
Salary Expense	600000	
Supplies Expense	22000	
Total Expense		1116000
Net Income		801000

Part IV (2)

Fowler's Crystal Palace
Capital Statement
For Year Ended December 31, 198—

Beginning Balance, Jan. 1		25525 00
Additional Investment		1000 00
		26525 00
Less: Withdrawals	12000 00	
Less Net Income	8010 00	
Decrease in Capital		3990 00
Ending Balance, Dec. 31		22535 00

Part IV (3)

Fowler's Crystal Palace
Balance Sheet
December 31, 198—

Assets		
Cash	2400 00	
Accounts Receivable	3850 00	
Merchandise Inventory	12080 00	
Furniture and Fixtures	8500 00	
Prepaid Insurance	100 00	
Supplies	105 00	
Total Assets		27035 00
Liabilities		
Accounts Payable		4500 00
Owner's Equity		
Dina Fowler, Capital		22535 00
Total Liabilities and Owner's Equity		27035 00

GENERAL JOURNAL   Page

cts. Pay. Dr.	General Dr.	Date		PR	General Cr.	Accts. Rec. Cr.
		198–	Adjusting Entries			
	1079000	Dec. 31	Revenue and Expense Summary			
			Merchandise Inventory		1079000	
	1208000	31	Merchandise Inventory			
			Revenue and Expense Summary		1208000	
	50000	31	Insurance Expense			
			Prepaid Insurance		50000	
	22000	31	Supplies Expense			
			Supplies		22000	
			Closing Entries			
	4059000	31	Sales			
	79500		Purchases Returns and Allowances			
			Revenue and Expense Summary		4138500	
	3466500	31	Revenue and Expense Summary			
			Sales Returns and Allowances		187500	
			Purchases		2163000	
			Advertising Expense		120000	
			Insurance Expense		50000	
			Miscellaneous Expense		24000	
			Rent Expense		300000	
			Salary Expense		600000	
			Supplies Expense		22000	
	801000	31	Revenue and Expense Summary			
			Dina Fowler, Capital		801000	
	1200000	31	Dina Fowler, Capital			
			Dina Fowler, Drawing		1200000	

INDEX

Account, 9, 23
Account form, (Balance sheet), 15
Accounts payable, 4, 119
Accounts receivable, 4, 137
Adjusting entry (adjustments), 171, 172, 197
Articles of partnership, 185
Asset, 3

Balance, 23, 47
Balance and rule, 77
Balance sheet, 15–16, 56, 66, 187
Bank reconciliation, 94–95
Bank statement, 94
Book of original entry, 29
Business transaction, 9

Cancelled check, 94
Capital, 6
Capital statement, 64, 185–186
Cash disbursements journal, 129–130
Cash receipts journal, 147
Chronological order, 40
Claims against assets, 15
Closing entry, 73, 199
Compound entry, 41
Controlling account, 122, 140
Correcting entry, 161
Cost of goods sold, 184–185
Credit (cr.), 23
Credit memorandum, 160
Creditor, 15
Cross referencing, 47

Debit (dr.), 23
Debit memorandum, 161
Deposit in transit, 94
Detail audit tape, 152
Disbursement, 102
Drawee, 91
Drawer, 91
Drawing account, 32
Double-entry bookkeeping/accounting, 25

Endorsement in blank, 91
Expenses, 31

Financial condition, 16
Fiscal period, 17
Footings, 47
Full endorsement (special), 92

General ledger, 120
Gross profit, 185

In balance, 47
Income statement, 56, 63, 184
Investment, 10

Journal, 39

Ledger, 23
Liabilities, 4

Merchandise, 119, 172

Net income, 31, 56
Net loss, 32, 56
Net worth, 5

On account, 119, 147
Outstanding checks, 94
Overdrawn, 95
Owner's equity, 5, 185

Partnership, 173, 185
Payee, 91
Petty cash, 101
Petty cash voucher, 102
Post-closing trial balance, 78, 200–201
Posting, 46
Prepaid expenses, 172
Profit, 31
Proprietorship, 5
Purchases journal, 119
Purchases returns and allowances, 159–160, 161

Qualified endorsement, 92

Replenish, 103–104
Report form (Balance sheet), 187
Restrictive endorsement, 92
Revenue, 31
Revenue and expense summary, 73, 199

Sales journal, 137–138
Sales returns and allowances, 159
Schedule of accounts payable, 122, 132
Schedule of accounts receivable, 140
Simple entry, 41
Statement of account, 162
Subsidiary ledger, 120

Summary entry (summarize), 120, 130, 148

T-account, 23
Trial Balance, 47, 171
Triplicate copy, 138

Valuation account, 160
Voucher, 102

Withdrawals, 32
Work sheet, 56, 174

Zero out, 73